CW00336656

harvest

To Katrina, Katie and Harriet
Ian

To Thelma,
my mother, a star
Penny

First published in 2004 by New Holland Publishers (NZ) Ltd
Auckland • Sydney • London • Cape Town

218 Lake Road, Northcote, Auckland, New Zealand
14 Aquatic Drive, Frenchs Forest, NSW 2086, Australia
86–88 Edgware Road, London W2 2EA, United Kingdom
80 McKenzie Street, Cape Town 8001, South Africa

www.newhollandpublishers.co.nz

Copyright © 2004 in text: Penny Oliver
Copyright © 2004 in photography: Ian Batchelor
Copyright © 2004 New Holland Publishers (NZ) Ltd

ISBN: 1 86966 049 8

Publishing manager: Renée Lang
Design: Christine Hansen
Editor: Barbara Nielsen

A catalogue record for this book is available from the National
Library of New Zealand.

10 9 8 7 6 5 4 3 2 1

Colour reproduction by Pica Digital, Singapore
Printed by Craft Print Pte Ltd

harvest

naturally good New Zealand food

FOOD BY PENNY OLIVER

PHOTOGRAPHY BY IAN BATCHELOR

NEW HOLLAND

Contents

Introduction

When I was growing up in Southland surrounded by a creative family that included assorted hunters, gatherers and passionate cooks, I learned to appreciate top-notch produce. It was a great foundation on which to build my culinary career. And it also provided the inspiration for my first cookbook, *Beach Bach Boat Barbecue* (with Ian Batchelor), a book that celebrated our unique summer lifestyle through lots of easy yet delicious meals that form an essential part of that lifestyle. The book that came next, *At Home At Play* (also with Ian), carried on the *Beach Bach…* tradition of matching food with outdoor activities, but this time gave equal emphasis to all four seasons.

Now, in *Harvest*, Ian and I focus on some of the best produce to be found in New Zealand – from succulent fresh fish and deliciously tender meat through to seasonal, lusciously ripe and full-flavoured fruit and vegetables. So many books these days put too much emphasis on dishes created with ingredients that originate on the other side of the world. But for the most part *Harvest* celebrates the wonderful key ingredients grown here in New Zealand – one of the cleanest places on earth. Our farm-raised beef and lamb; the fish and shellfish hauled up from the depths of our clear blue seas; and our fantastic fruit, vegetables and dairy products, harvested from our uniquely beautiful land, remain the envy of the rest of the world.

Now a brief word about the recipes that embrace these fabulous ingredients. Some of them are 'traditional with a twist', while others have been influenced by the impact of the Pacific-rim cuisine that can now be spotted on so many café and restaurant menus these days and which we all enjoy so much. But the really important thing to know about *Harvest* is that the focus is always on choosing good quality, fresh ingredients that naturally give great taste and flavour.

It remains for me to say that after browsing through these recipes and Ian Batchelor's sublime food photography, I hope you'll be inspired to think about what's in season right now – and start cooking!

Penny Oliver

from the sea

fish

Whitebait Salad on Coriander Omelettes

WHITEBAIT SALAD

2½ cups finely shredded Savoy cabbage

½ cup fresh basil leaves, finely shredded

½ cup fresh mint leaves, finely shredded

2 fresh kaffir lime leaves, finely shredded

½ cup raw peanuts, roasted and chopped

1 large fresh red chilli, deseeded and finely chopped

200g whitebait, rinsed, drained and dried

4 tablespoons plain flour

vegetable oil

DRESSING

¼ cup lime juice

2 tablespoons fish sauce

1 tablespoon grated palm sugar

1 clove garlic, peeled and grated

1 teaspoon grated fresh ginger

Place the cabbage, basil, mint, lime leaves, peanuts and chilli in a bowl and toss together. Place the whitebait in a plastic bag with the flour and shake together to lightly coat the whitebait with flour. Shake off the excess flour. Heat the vegetable oil in a frying pan to a medium-high heat. Cook the whitebait in batches until it browns, then drain on absorbent kitchen paper. Keep warm.

Shake together all the ingredients for the dressing, drizzle it over the salad and toss together.

CORIANDER OMELETTES

6 large eggs, beaten

2 tablespoons milk

sea salt to taste

¼ cup fresh coriander leaves, chopped

olive oil

Beat together the eggs, milk, salt and coriander. Lightly grease a 16–18cm crêpe pan with olive oil and place over a medium-high heat. Allow 2 tablespoons of batter per omelette. Pour 2 tablespoons of batter into the centre of the pan and tilt it to spread the mixture over the bottom of the pan. Cook for 1 minute or until the underside is browning and the batter is set. Turn and cook the other side. Continue until all the batter is used.

Pile the salad onto the omelettes and top with the whitebait. Serve immediately.

SERVES 6

Cod in Coconut Sauce
Any combination of thick, meaty fillets of fish will work in this silky coconut cream sauce – hapuku or orange roughy are particularly good.

1 tablespoon vegetable oil
1 shallot (eschallot), finely chopped
1 clove garlic, peeled and grated
1 fresh red chilli, deseeded and finely chopped
400ml coconut cream
1 tablespoon lime juice
1 tablespoon fish sauce
2 teaspoons grated palm sugar
1 stalk lemon grass, white part only, finely sliced
800g cod fillet, cut into 6 portions
¼ cup fresh chopped coriander leaves

Place the vegetable oil, shallot and garlic in a frying pan and fry over a gentle heat until soft. Add the chilli, coconut cream, lime juice, fish sauce, palm sugar and the lemon grass and simmer gently for 5 minutes. Place the pieces of fish in the pan, cover with a lid and cook for 3–4 minutes each side until just cooked. Stir the coriander through and serve with a little Cucumber Salad (below) and noodles or jasmine rice.

SERVES 6

Cucumber Salad

1 telegraph cucumber, peeled
1 tablespoon salt
1 tablespoon lime juice
1 tablespoon fish sauce
grated palm sugar to taste

Cut the cucumber in half lengthways and remove all the seeds. Using a vegetable peeler, peel strips from the cucumber flesh, or slice it finely, and place in a bowl. Sprinkle the salt over and mix together well. Let it stand for 20 minutes, then wash off the salt and drain on absorbent kitchen paper. Place the cucumber in a clean bowl, add the lime juice, fish sauce and palm sugar to taste and gently combine.

Cod in Coconut Sauce

Tuna and Avocado Tartare The fresher the tuna the better you will appreciate its dense, rich texture and flavour, especially when mixed with aromatic summer herbs, lemon and avocado.

1 telegraph cucumber, skinned
400g yellow fin tuna
1 firm, ripe avocado
4 tablespoons lime juice
2 tablespoons extra virgin olive oil
¼ cup fresh basil leaves, shredded
½ cup fresh mint leaves, shredded
sea salt and freshly ground black pepper to taste

Cut the cucumber in half lengthways and remove the seeds. Dice the flesh into small pieces. Dice the tuna into even-sized pieces. Halve the avocado and remove the stone. Peel off the skin and dice the flesh. Place all the diced ingredients into a bowl. Drizzle with the lime juice and extra virgin olive oil. Gently toss the herbs and seasonings through. Chill in the fridge for 15 minutes. Serve in small bowls accompanied by thin slices of grilled bread.

SERVES 6

Wood-roasted Salmon with Puy Lentils

Rose pink and rich, wood-roasted salmon is available in most supermarkets. Gently tossed with quick-to-cook French green lentils from Puy, it makes an impressive and easily prepared healthy lunch.

2 cups Puy lentils
3 eggs, hard-boiled and shelled
¹/₂ red onion, peeled and finely chopped
³/₄ cup finely chopped fresh flat-leaf parsley
1 avocado, peeled, stoned and diced
sea salt and freshly ground black pepper to taste
squeeze of lemon juice to taste
¹/₈ cup avocado oil
200g wood-roasted salmon, divided into small chunks

Simmer the lentils in plenty of salted water for 15 minutes or until tender, drain and dry on absorbent kitchen paper, then place in a bowl. Quarter the eggs and place in the bowl of lentils with the onion, parsley, avocado, seasonings, lemon juice, avocado oil and salmon and gently toss together.

SERVES 6

Wood-roasted Salmon with Puy Lentils

Salmon Carpaccio

For an alluring starter, simply overlap thin slices of creamy raw salmon on a large platter and adorn with a smattering of Asian tastes.

600g salmon fillet, pin boned
2½ tablespoons mirin
1½ tablespoons soy sauce
1 teaspoon lemon juice
1 teaspoon sesame oil
1 teaspoon grated fresh ginger
1 teaspoon grated palm sugar
fresh chopped chives
1 pickled lemon, flesh removed

Slice the salmon thinly towards the tail end. Arrange the slices on serving plates or one large platter. Mix together the mirin, soy sauce, lemon juice, sesame oil, ginger and palm sugar. Spoon the dressing over the salmon. Sprinkle with the chives. Lastly, finely slice the pickled lemon skin and use to garnish.

SERVES 6

Oyster Omelette

PER PERSON:

2–3 organic eggs
1 tablespoon water
1 tablespoon cream
olive oil
butter
4–6 plump oysters, preferably Bluff
1 tablespoon chopped chives
freshly ground black pepper to taste
squeeze of lemon juice
fresh salmon roe to garnish

Place the eggs, water and cream in a bowl and whisk together. Put a little olive oil and a knob of butter in a pan over a medium heat and heat until the butter becomes nutty, then pour in the egg mixture. Quickly pull the sides of the omelette in with a fork as it cooks to allow the liquid egg to replace the cooked egg. When the egg is still loose and moist, place the oysters down the middle of the omelette, sprinkle with the chives and pepper and squeeze some lemon juice over. Fold the sides over the oysters and form a torpedo-shaped omelette. Serve immediately with a wedge of lemon, a spoonful of salmon roe and a crisp salad, for lunch or supper.

Scallops and Lemon Butter Sauce

For a sensational lunch dish, try these soft seared

scallops with a traditional lemon-flavoured butter sauce,

contrasted with crunchy lettuce and crisp prosciutto.

LEMON BUTTER SAUCE
4 tablespoons fresh lemon juice
120ml chicken stock
300g butter, cubed and chilled
sea salt to taste

Place the lemon juice and chicken stock in a saucepan and heat
to boiling point. Lower the temperature and maintain the heat
just under boiling point. Whisk in the chilled butter cubes a
few pieces at a time until they melt and the sauce thickens.
Add sea salt to taste. Keep warm.

MAKES ABOUT 1 1/2 CUPS

SCALLOPS
4 tablespoons olive oil for frying
1kg scallops, coral (roe) on
12 slices prosciutto, grilled crisp
crisp lettuce, washed and dried

Heat a frying pan over a high heat with a little olive oil. Begin
to cook the scallops in batches for 1–2 minutes on each side.
Arrange the lettuce, scallops and crispy prosciutto on serving
plates and drizzle with the lemon butter sauce. Serve
immediately.

SERVES 6

Scallops and Lemon Butter Sauce

Shellfish Chowder

Shellfish Chowder Full of bold seafood flavours, this traditional, sumptuous chowder is a meal on its own.

600g clams, cleaned

600g small mussels, cleaned

1 cup dry white wine

1 bay leaf

2 sprigs fresh thyme

1 clove garlic, peeled and crushed

2 small red onions, finely chopped

6 rashers bacon, finely diced

1 tablespoon olive oil

3 Agria potatoes, peeled and finely diced

3 cups fish or chicken stock

$1\frac{1}{2}$ cups cream

2 teaspoons freshly grated lemon zest

sea salt and freshly ground black pepper to taste

18 scallops, coral (roe) on

crab claws to garnish

flat-leaf parsley to garnish

Place the clams and mussels in a large saucepan with the white wine, bay leaf and thyme. Cover the saucepan and cook the shellfish over a medium heat until they open. Discard any unopened shellfish. Remove the shellfish from the liquid, strain the cooking liquid and set aside. When cool, remove the meat from the shells. Cook the garlic, onion and bacon in the olive oil over a low heat until soft. Add the potatoes, reserved shellfish liquid and the stock. Cover and simmer until the potatoes are just tender.

Remove from the heat and stir in the cream, lemon zest and seasonings to taste. Drop in the clams, mussels, scallops and crab claws, the parsley and a few clam and mussel shells to garnish the soup. Cook for 1 minute, then serve in bowls with a hearty sourdough bread.

SERVES 6

Fried Mussels and Red Pepper Sauce

RED PEPPER SAUCE

2 tablespoons olive oil

1 leek, thinly sliced

2 cloves garlic, peeled

2 red peppers (capsicums), deseeded and sliced

1 tablespoon tomato paste

sea salt and freshly ground black pepper to taste

12 large mussels, steamed open and removed from shells

plain flour

extra virgin olive oil

fresh coriander sprigs to garnish

lemon wedges for serving

Heat the olive oil in a saucepan over a gentle heat and fry the sliced leek until soft. Add the garlic, peppers, tomato paste and seasonings. Spoon mixture into an ovenproof dish, cover with aluminium foil and bake in a preheated oven at 180°C for 20 minutes until the red peppers are soft. Cool, then process in a blender until puréed and smooth. Taste and adjust seasonings if necessary.

Dust the mussels with flour and fry them in medium-hot extra virgin olive oil for 2–3 minutes until crisp and golden. To serve, spoon the warm sauce onto each plate. Top with two fried mussels, garnish with fresh coriander sprigs and serve with a wedge of lemon.

SERVES 6

Grilled Hapuku on Potato Stew
Firm-fleshed white fish such as hapuku holds together well when grilled, making it ideal for serving on top of this tasty, peasant-style stew.

STEW

1 tablespoon butter

1 tablespoon olive oil

2 spring onions, finely sliced

2 cloves garlic, peeled and grated

1 tablespoon good-quality bought basil pesto

8 waxy potatoes, peeled and diced

800ml chicken stock

4 vine-ripened tomatoes, finely chopped

sea salt and freshly ground black pepper to taste

½ cup black olives, pitted

6 x 150g hapuku steaks

extra virgin olive oil

¼ cup finely chopped fresh flat-leaf parsley

lemon wedges to garnish

Melt the butter and olive oil together in a saucepan over a medium heat. Add the spring onions, garlic and pesto and cook for 2 minutes. Add the diced potatoes and fry for 5 minutes. Add the chicken stock and cook gently for 15–20 minutes or until the potatoes are just tender and some of the stock is absorbed. Add the tomatoes, seasonings and olives and continue to cook for 5 minutes until the tomatoes soften and the stock has thickened slightly.

Brush the hapuku steaks generously with extra virgin olive oil. Place the hapuku on a hot grill or barbecue and cook for 2–3 minutes each side. Stir the parsley through the stew and place spoonfuls in the centre of each plate. Rest the hapuku on top and drizzle with a little extra virgin olive oil. Garnish with the lemon wedges.

SERVES 6

Grilled Squid Salad

Grilled Squid Salad A hot grill and short cooking time are the secrets to successful squid cooking. This combination of squid, peppery rocket leaves, colourful, juicy tomatoes and a sharp sherry dressing makes a refreshing first course.

600g squid tubes
sea salt and freshly ground black pepper to taste
rocket leaves
watercress leaves
24 vine-ripened cherry tomatoes, halved
Sherry Vinaigrette (see recipe on page 36)

Using a sharp knife, split the squid tubes open and score the skin in a crisscross pattern. Sprinkle with the seasonings. Cook the squid in a hot ridged grill pan for a minute each side, then slice. Toss the warm squid, rocket leaves, watercress and tomatoes together in a bowl. Drizzle with enough dressing to moisten and flavour the salad. Pile onto plates and serve immediately.

SERVES 6

Smoked Eel with Watercress Pesto on Grilled Sourdough

12 slices sourdough bread
olive oil
2 cloves garlic, peeled
1 1/2 tightly packed cups watercress leaves
1/2 cup pine nuts
1/4 teaspoon sea salt
1 tablespoon lemon juice
1/4 cup extra virgin olive oil
400g smoked eel (bought)
freshly ground black pepper

Brush the sourdough bread with olive oil on both sides and lightly grill each side until the crust is crispy but the bread inside still has a chewy texture. Place the garlic, watercress, pine nuts, salt, and lemon juice in a food processor and, with the motor running, drizzle in the extra virgin olive oil to form a smooth, thick pesto. Spread the grilled sourdough with a little watercress pesto and place some smoked eel on top. Finish with a grinding of black pepper.

MAKES 12

Mussel, Zucchini and Almond Fritters

1 cup cooked mussel meat, beards removed, flesh
  chopped
3 large zucchini (courgettes), grated
2 cloves garlic, peeled and grated
3 spring onions, finely sliced
grated zest of 1 lemon
³/₄ cup blanched almonds, roasted and chopped
¹/₂ cup plain flour
2 eggs, beaten
sea salt and freshly ground black pepper to taste
olive oil for cooking
lemon wedges and crème fraîche for serving

Place the mussel meat, zucchini, garlic, spring onions, lemon
zest, almonds, flour, eggs and seasonings in a bowl and mix
together until well combined. Fry spoonfuls of the mixture in
olive oil over a medium-high heat until cooked and golden
brown on both sides. Serve at once with lemon wedges and a
dollop of crème fraîche.

MAKES 12 SMALL FRITTERS

Coconut Prawns
These look spectacular and make delicious bite-sized morsels, hot from the pan, to serve with drinks.

1kg large green prawns, shelled, deveined, tails on
plain flour
3 egg whites, lightly beaten
2 cups shredded coconut
vegetable oil

Dip the prawns into the flour to lightly coat, shake off the excess flour, then dip them into the beaten egg white mixture, followed by the coconut. Lay them on a plate and refrigerate for 20 minutes.

Heat the vegetable oil in a frying pan over a medium heat. Cook the prawns a few at a time for 2–3 minutes each side until golden. Drain on absorbent kitchen paper. Serve with mayonnaise (see recipe for Lemon Mayonnaise on page 137) or an Asian dipping sauce.

MAKES ABOUT 20 PRAWNS

Coconut Prawns

Crayfish on Mango Ricotta Cakes

Tender pieces of crayfish and mango flavoured with mint, lime and the heat of red chilli festoon these light, tasty ricotta cakes – perfect for a celebratory lunch.

RICOTTA CAKES

175g ricotta cheese

75g fresh parmesan cheese, grated

75g feta cheese, crumbled

sea salt and freshly ground black pepper to taste

finely grated zest of 1 lemon

2 tablespoons chopped fresh flat-leaf parsley

2 tablespoons plain flour

extra flour

olive oil

Place all three cheeses, seasonings, lemon zest, parsley and flour together in a bowl and mix well. Divide the mixture into 6 equal-sized cakes. Dip the cakes into the extra flour to lightly coat them. In a frying pan heat a little olive oil to a medium-high heat and cook the cakes three at a time until golden on both sides.

CRAYFISH

3 baby crayfish tails, cooked and shelled

2 mangoes, peeled

1 fresh red chilli, deseeded and thinly sliced

$\frac{1}{2}$ cup fresh mint, finely chopped

2 tablespoons lime juice

Cut the crayfish tails into bite-sized slices. Remove the flesh from the peeled mango by cutting it from the stone, then slice evenly. Add the chilli, mint and lime juice and gently mix together. To serve, lay slices of the mango mixture on top of the ricotta cakes and top with the crayfish.

SERVES 6

Crayfish on Mango Ricotta Cakes

from the farm

meat

Tarragon and Lemon Chicken with Baby Onions

French tarragon, with its distinctive anise-like flavour, should always be used in this dish in preference to its Russian 'cousin'.

12 corn-fed chicken thighs on the bone, skin on

3 cloves garlic, peeled and grated

sea salt and freshly ground black pepper to taste

1½ cups finely chopped French tarragon leaves

1 tablespoon grated lemon zest

1 tablespoon lemon juice

200g unsalted butter, softened

24 small brown pickling onions, peeled and halved

¼ cup olive oil

fresh tarragon sprigs

Pat the chicken dry with absorbent kitchen paper. Place the garlic, seasonings, chopped tarragon, lemon zest, lemon juice and butter in a bowl and beat together until well combined or pulse together in a food processor. Using your fingers, loosen and lift the skin from the flesh of the chicken, spread some tarragon butter under the skin, then pat the skin back into place. Transfer the remaining butter to a ramekin, seal with plastic food wrap and refrigerate until ready to use later.

Place the chicken thighs in a baking dish and scatter the onions around them. Drizzle with the olive oil and scatter some of the extra sprigs of tarragon on them. Bake in a preheated oven at 180°C for 1 hour. Turn the onions halfway through cooking and baste the chicken.

Transfer the chicken to a serving plate and spoon the onions and juices around it. Slice up the refrigerated tarragon butter and rub it over the top of the chicken. Garnish with some sprigs of fresh tarragon and serve.

SERVES 6

Pork, Crackling and Herb Salsa

2¹/₂–3kg rolled pork loin, skin on, finely scored (cuts about 5mm apart)

olive oil and sea salt for rubbing

2 cloves garlic, peeled

2 tablespoons capers, rinsed

¹/₂ cup coarsely chopped sweet pickled gherkins

6 anchovy fillets

2 tightly packed cups fresh flat-leaf parsley

1 tightly packed cup fresh basil leaves

¹/₂ tightly packed cup fresh mint leaves

¹/₂ tightly packed cup fresh thyme leaves

1 teaspoon Dijon mustard

sea salt and freshly ground black pepper to taste

2 tablespoons red wine vinegar

extra virgin olive oil to mix

Ensure the pork skin is well scored. Ask your butcher to increase the surface scoring if this is not already done. Rub the skin well with olive oil and salt. Place the garlic, capers, gherkins, anchovy fillets, herbs, mustard, seasonings and vinegar in a food processor and pulse to chop. With the motor running, drizzle in the extra virgin olive oil until you have a fragrant, thick paste.

Roast the pork in a preheated oven at 220°C for 30 minutes, then turn the oven down to 180°C and continue to roast for a further 40 minutes. If you wish to crackle the skin further, place the meat under a medium-hot grill for a few minutes. Rest the roast for 10–15 minutes before you carve it. Serve slices of pork crackling with a spoonful of herb salsa on the side.

SERVES 6–8

Pork Ribs   Use full-length ribs as they look sculptural and dramatic piled onto a large white serving plate steaming with Chinese scents.

MARINADE

6 tablespoons soy sauce

6 tablespoons tomato sauce (ketchup)

¼ cup lemon juice

3 tablespoons brown sugar

3 tablespoons liquid honey

3 tablespoons sweet sherry

3 tablespoons hoisin sauce

3 cloves garlic, peeled and grated

1 fresh red 'bird's eye' chilli, finely chopped

2 tablespoons olive oil

2kg (about 4 racks) pork spareribs, cut into single ribs

Mix together the marinade ingredients. Place the spareribs in a shallow dish just large enough to hold them. Thoroughly coat the ribs with the marinade, cover and refrigerate for at least 3 hours (preferably overnight), turning the ribs occasionally.

Place the marinated ribs on an oiled barbecue grill over a medium heat. Grill, basting occasionally with the marinade, for about 7–10 minutes each side or until the meat is opaque, golden and still juicy. Pile the ribs onto a serving plate.

SERVES 6–8

Pickled Pork

1½–2kg rolled pickled pork shoulder

1 onion, peeled and studded with 6 whole cloves

1 bay leaf

2 carrots, sliced

fresh parsley sprigs

fresh thyme sprigs

Place the pork in a large stock pot and cover with cold water. Add the onion, bay leaf, carrots and herb sprigs. Cover and bring to the boil. Reduce the heat to a simmer. Remove the lid slightly so the pot is only partially covered and cook for 1½–2 hours until the meat is tender. To serve the meat hot, leave it sitting in the liquid until ready to slice. If you serve it cold, leave it to cool in the liquid, then remove and refrigerate, covered, until ready to slice.

SERVES 6–8

Chicken Sandwiches Deluxe What could be more

delicious than a moist gourmet sandwich, guaranteed to impress.

2 medium chickens, boiled or bought ready-cooked, or 1kg chicken
    breasts, poached, skinned, meat removed and cut into bite-sized
    pieces
homemade whole-egg mayonnaise (see recipe for Lemon Mayonnaise
    on page 137) or a favourite bought one
$^1/_4$ cup chopped fresh flat-leaf parsley
2 cups thinly sliced young celery
$^1/_2$ cup toasted pine nuts
sea salt and freshly ground black pepper to taste
2 loaves sliced brown bread
softened butter
2 firm ripe avocados, peeled, stoned and thinly sliced
watercress or rocket leaves

If using boiled or bought ready-cooked chicken, remove the meat from the bones.
Place the chicken meat in a bowl. Spoon in enough mayonnaise to make the chicken
very moist. Add the parsley, celery, pine nuts and seasonings and combine well. Butter
half the bread right to the edges. Divide the mixture generously and evenly over the
bread. Place 2–3 slices of avocado over the top and a few sprigs of watercress or some
rocket leaves on top of the avocado. Top with another layer of buttered bread. Press
down gently but firmly and wrap in plastic food wrap. Refrigerate for at least 1 hour.

    Remove from the fridge 1 hour before serving and cut off the crusts. If you have an
electric bread knife, you can cut three sandwich rounds at a time. Cut each sandwich
into three fingers. Arrange on a serving plate, cover with plastic food wrap and leave
in a cool place until ready to serve. Serve at room temperature, garnished with sprigs
of watercress.

MAKES ABOUT 66 FINGERS

Chicken Sandwiches Deluxe

Chicken Stuffed with Ham, Herbs and Pistachio

If the occasion calls for cold chicken, then serve this savoury terrine-style chicken dish, which was a favourite back in my catering days.

1 small onion, peeled and finely chopped
1 clove garlic, peeled and finely chopped
1 tablespoon olive oil
1 cup finely chopped leg ham
1 cup fresh white breadcrumbs
1/2 cup chopped pistachio nuts
1/2 cup fresh flat-leaf parsley, finely chopped
2 tablespoons basil pesto (homemade or bought)
1 egg
sea salt and freshly ground black pepper to taste
6 slices prosciutto
1 large chicken, boned (you could ask your butcher to do this)

Fry the onion and garlic in the olive oil over a low heat until soft. Allow to cool, then add the ham, breadcrumbs, pistachios, parsley, pesto, egg and seasonings. Stir well to combine. Line a 20cm-long loaf tin with the slices of prosciutto. Lay the chicken skin-side down on a board. Place the stuffing in a sausage shape down the middle of the chicken then fold the sides over. Place the chicken in the loaf tin, folded-side down, then fold the prosciutto over the top. Bake in a preheated oven at 180°C for 1$\frac{1}{4}$–1$\frac{1}{2}$ hours or until the juices run clear when a skewer is inserted. Allow to cool in the tin before removing and slicing.

SERVES 8

Oven-roasted Lamb Knuckles Lamb knuckles or shanks require long, slow, wet roasting, which results in succulent, tender meat. The crunchy breadcrumb and pecorino crust gives a delicious contrast.

6 well-trimmed lamb shanks or knuckles

100ml olive oil

1 cup finely chopped fresh flat-leaf parsley

$^1/_2$ cup finely chopped fresh sage leaves

$^1/_4$ cup finely chopped fresh rosemary leaves

4 cloves garlic, peeled and grated

1 fresh red chilli, deseeded and finely chopped

freshly ground black pepper

1 red onion, finely chopped

2 tomatoes, finely chopped

1 bay leaf

300ml white wine

1 litre chicken stock

$^3/_4$ cup fresh breadcrumbs

$^1/_2$ cup grated pecorino cheese

Place the lamb shanks in a deep roasting dish. Sprinkle with the olive oil, parsley, sage, rosemary, garlic, chilli and pepper. Massage this mixture into the meat with your finger tips. Add the onion, tomatoes, bay leaf, white wine and chicken stock. Roast in a preheated oven at 180°C for 1 hour, then turn the meat over. Sprinkle the shanks with the breadcrumbs and pecorino cheese. Continue to roast for 1 more hour. When the meat is tender, transfer from the pan to a serving platter. Spoon the pan contents around the meat and serve.

SERVES 6

Lamb Cutlets with a Zatar Crust

Also known as Za'atar or Zahtar, this Middle Eastern culinary herb mix includes dried thyme, sumac and toasted sesame seeds and is available from most delicatessens. Mixed with a little olive oil and lemon juice, zatar is also delicious stirred into a thick paste and spread on grilled breads.

8 tablespoons zatar
2 tablespoons finely chopped fresh flat-leaf parsley
olive oil
18 lamb cutlets

Combine the zatar, parsley and enough olive oil to make a thick paste. Lay the lamb cutlets on a flat surface and spread both sides of the cutlets with the zatar paste. Grill or pan fry for 5–7 minutes each side for rare; 7–10 minutes for medium; and 10–12 minutes if you like them well cooked (but be careful that you don't let them become dry). Serve with Pickled Walnut and Ebly Salad (see recipe on page 72).

SERVES 6

Lamb Cutlets with a Zatar Crust

Venison Patties

800g minced lean venison
½ cup freshly grated white breadcrumbs
¼ cup finely grated parmesan cheese
¼ cup canned cranberry sauce
1 teaspoon Dijon mustard
1 teaspoon grated lemon zest
2 cloves garlic, peeled and grated
¼ cup finely chopped fresh chives
1 small egg
sea salt and freshly ground black pepper to taste
olive oil for cooking

Place all the ingredients in a bowl and thoroughly mix together. Using wet hands shape the mixture into balls and flatten into patties. Either grill under a medium-high grill until golden and cooked, or fry in batches in a large frying pan over a medium-high heat with a little olive oil to prevent sticking, for 5–7 minutes each side. Drain on absorbent kitchen paper and serve.

SERVES 6

Rosemary and Lemon-infused Lamb

MARINADE
3 cloves garlic, peeled and grated
fresh rosemary leaves, chopped
lemon-infused extra virgin olive oil

2kg butterflied leg of lamb (ask your butcher to do this)
sea salt and freshly ground black pepper to taste

Mix together the garlic, rosemary and lemon-infused extra virgin olive oil. Lay the lamb on a flat surface and, using a sharp knife, score the surface of the meat in a crisscross pattern on both sides. Rub the marinade into the scored surfaces and work it into the meat. Allow to sit and marinate for 1 hour before cooking.

When ready to roast, place a little oil in the bottom of a roasting pan and add the meat. Season with salt and pepper and roast in a preheated oven at 200–225°C. Turn halfway through cooking and season again. When cooked, remove from the oven and let it stand for 15 minutes before carving.

Cooking times:
For pink lamb allow about 1 hour
For medium lamb allow about 1¼ hours
For well-done lamb allow about 1½ hours

SERVES 6–8

Peking Duck Rolls

The gamey flavour of duck marries well with Asian sauces, crisp vegetables and fresh, aromatic herbs. Rice wrappers make for convenient handling of these delicious morsels, and if it's a casual occasion, invite your guests to help make them up.

$^3/_4$ cup hoisin sauce

$^1/_4$ cup rice vinegar

1 teaspoon peeled and grated fresh ginger

1 tablespoon fresh orange juice

1 small fresh red 'bird's eye' chilli, deseeded and very finely chopped

300g bought roasted Peking duck, cut into strips

1 medium carrot, peeled and cut into about 20 thin strips about 5cm long

$^1/_2$ telegraph cucumber, peeled, cored and cut into 20 thin strips
   about 5cm long

4 spring onions, cut into 20 strips about 5cm long

$^1/_2$ cup fresh coriander leaves

$^1/_2$ cup fresh mint leaves

20 large rice paper wrappers

Place the hoisin sauce, rice vinegar, ginger, orange juice and chilli in a bowl and combine. Place the duck in a bowl with half the sauce mixture and stir to coat the duck well. Line up the strips of carrot, telegraph cucumber, spring onions and the herbs in order of use. Soak the rice paper wrappers one at a time in a bowl of hot water until just softened, shake off the excess water and lay on a damp, clean tea-towel. Remembering to divide the filling equally among the rolls, place two strips of duck and a proportion of the remaining filling ingredients on top near one side of the wrapper. Fold over one side and then roll up to enclose, leaving one side open so you see the inside filling. Keep the rolls covered with a damp tea-towel while you make the rest. Serve the rolls with the remaining sauce on the side or in a small bowl for dipping.

MAKES 20

Roast of Beef with Horseradish and Popovers

ROAST BEEF

1.5kg beef fillet, trimmed

kitchen string

2 tablespoons olive oil

sea salt to taste

Tuck under the thin end of the beef and tie with kitchen string to secure. Continue to tie the string around the fillet at 3–4cm intervals. Place the fillet in a non-stick roasting pan and rub the olive oil and salt over the meat. Roast in a preheated oven at 220°C for 20–30 minutes for a medium-rare result. Rest for 10 minutes before carving.

HOT HORSERADISH SAUCE

2 fresh horseradish roots, peeled and grated or minced

¼ cup good quality bought horseradish

1 teaspoon powdered hot English mustard

water

½ cup crème fraîche

Place the fresh and bought horseradish in a small bowl. Mix the mustard with enough water to make a smooth paste and pour it into the horseradish. Add the crème fraîche and stir all the ingredients together.

SERVES 6–8

Yorkshire Pudding Popovers

4 tablespoons lard

2 eggs

1 cup milk

⅔ cup plain flour, sifted

Preheat the oven to 220°C. Place 1 teaspoon of lard in 12 x ½-cup capacity muffin pans and heat in the oven to melt the lard. Whisk together the eggs and milk until combined, then gradually add the flour, whisking as you go to make a smooth batter. Remove the muffin pans from the oven. Place 2 tablespoons of batter into each pan. Bake for 30 minutes or until puffed and golden.

MAKES 12

Roast of Beef with Horseradish and Popovers

Poached Fillet of Beef in Prosciutto Prosciutto

wrapped around the beef salts and enriches the poaching stock and also

gives a lovely finish to the appearance of the beef when cut and plated.

Bean Stew (see recipe on page 70) is a great accompaniment to this dish.

2 x 800g pieces scotch or eye fillet, well trimmed

28–30 thin slices prosciutto

fresh thyme sprigs

fresh rosemary sprigs

kitchen string

3 cups veal or beef stock

2 cups chicken stock

1 cup red wine

Lay half the prosciutto slices slightly overlapping on a clean work surface. Lay the beef in the centre and wrap the prosciutto around the beef to enclose it. Repeat for the second piece. Tie the prosciutto around the beef at 2–4cm intervals, tucking in a piece of rosemary or thyme beneath the string as you go. Place the beef in a casserole or poaching pan just big enough to snugly fit the meat. Pour in enough stock and wine to just cover the meat. Cover with a lid and place on the heat. Bring to a simmer, then turn down so that the liquid just simmers for 20 minutes for a rare result. Allow another 5–10 minutes for medium. When cooked to your liking, remove the meat from the stock and allow it to rest for 10–15 minutes before carving.

If you like, put the stock through a fine sieve and freeze for use in flavouring stews and casseroles.

SERVES 12

Spiced Sausage, Apple and Onion Tart

Spiced Sausage, Apple and Onion Tart A classic

combination but don't stint on the sausages! – good-quality spiced

sausages are essential to the success of this dish.

PASTRY

250g plain flour

100g chilled butter, cubed

2 egg yolks

2–3 tablespoons chilled water

Place the flour and butter in a food processor and process to a fine crumb. Add the egg yolks and enough water to process the mixture to a firm ball of dough. Wrap in plastic food wrap and refrigerate for 30 minutes. When you are ready to assemble the tart, roll the dough out to fit a 23cm loose-bottomed tart tin or an equivalent-sized oblong tart tin. Ease the dough into the tin, trim the edge and place the pastry-lined tin back in the fridge until ready to fill.

FILLING

1 red onion, peeled, halved and sliced

2 medium sweet red-skinned apples, cored and sliced

1 tablespoon olive oil

3–4 chorizo sausages, grilled and sliced

3 eggs

$\frac{1}{2}$ cup milk

1$\frac{1}{4}$ cups cream

$\frac{1}{2}$ cup grated pecorino cheese

Cook the onion and apples in a frying pan with the olive oil until soft. Arrange evenly over the bottom of the tart case in the tin. Lay the sliced cooked sausages evenly over the top. Beat together the eggs, milk and cream and pour over the filling. Sprinkle with the cheese. Bake in a preheated oven at 200°C for 35–40 minutes until just set and golden. Serve with Plum and Apple Chutney (see recipe on page 136).

SERVES 6

Orange and Spiced-lamb Salad Sweet and sour citrus flavours complement the juicy spiced lamb in this light dish, which is pefect as a starter or a lunch.

SPICE PASTE

1½ teaspoons black peppercorns

1½ teaspoons cumin seeds

1 teaspoon coriander seeds

1 teaspoon yellow mustard seeds

2 dried chillies, deseeded and sliced

4 cloves garlic, peeled and chopped

1 small red onion, peeled and sliced

¼ cup fresh coriander leaves

¼ cup fresh flat-leaf parsley leaves

sea salt to taste

olive oil

600g lamb fillets

200g salad greens of choice

3 sweet navel, Seville or blood oranges

DRESSING

3 tablespoons extra virgin olive oil

2 tablespoons fresh lime juice

1 clove garlic, peeled and grated

1 red chilli, deseeded and very finely chopped

Place the peppercorns, cumin seeds, coriander seeds, mustard seeds and chillies in a saucepan and dry roast over a medium heat until the seeds begin to pop. Cool, then crush with a pestle and mortar or pulse them in a blender or food processor. Add the garlic, onion, fresh coriander and parsley leaves and seasonings and blend to a spreadable paste with olive oil.

Spread the paste over the lamb and marinate for 1 hour in the fridge. Grill the lamb on a medium to high heat until cooked to your liking. Allow the lamb to stand for 10 minutes before carving. To serve, slice the lamb and mix with your choice of salad leaves and the orange segments. Combine all the dressing ingredients and drizzle over the salad just before serving.

SERVES 6

Shoulder of Lamb with Herb Anchovy Sauce

This old-fashioned tender cut of lamb is one of my all-time favourites. The intense, flavoursome sauce provides a wonderful contrast to the meat.

2 x 2kg 'oyster' shoulders

12 cloves garlic, peeled and coarsely chopped

8 tablespoons fresh rosemary leaves, coarsely chopped

4 tablespoons lemon juice

1/2 cup olive oil

freshly ground black pepper

6 tablespoons sea salt

1 1/2 cups Herb Anchovy Sauce (see recipe below)

Use a sharp knife to score the surface of the lamb in a crisscross pattern. To make the marinade, place the garlic, rosemary, lemon juice and olive oil in a food processor and pulse together to combine. Place the lamb in a shallow dish and paste the marinade over. Marinate for an hour, turning halfway through.

Place the shoulder and marinade in a roasting pan and season with pepper. Roast in a preheated oven at 200°C for 20 minutes. Sprinkle the salt over and roast for a further 30–35 minutes at 170°C until crusty and brown. Serve with a couple of dollops of Herb Anchovy Sauce on the side.

SERVES 8

Herb Anchovy Sauce

2 packed cups fresh flat-leaf parsley

1 1/4 packed cups fresh tarragon

1 packed cup fresh mint

2 cloves garlic, peeled

1 teaspoon capers, rinsed

2–3 anchovies

3–4 tablespoons red wine vinegar

6–8 tablespoons extra virgin olive oil

freshly ground black pepper

squeeze of lemon juice

sea salt to taste

Roughly chop the parsley, tarragon and mint. Place all the ingredients in a food processor and blend to a thick sauce.

MAKES 1 1/2 CUPS

Veal, Pork and Chicken Roulade
Don't be daunted by the long list of ingredients. This is a simply prepared recipe for a savoury charcuterie treat to pack in a picnic or entertain friends.

1 tablespoon olive oil

1 onion, peeled and finely chopped

2 cloves garlic, peeled and grated

250g minced veal

250g minced pork

1 cup fresh breadcrumbs

1 egg

¼ cup brandy

¼ cup chopped fresh flat-leaf parsley

⅛ cup chopped fresh sage leaves

sea salt and freshly ground black pepper to taste

12 thin slices pancetta

4 skinless corn-fed chicken breasts

fresh basil leaves

10–12 thin slices ham

5 small eggs, hard-boiled and shelled

Heat the olive oil in a frying pan over a medium heat and cook the onion and garlic until soft. In a large bowl mix together the minced veal and pork, breadcrumbs, egg, brandy, parsley, sage, seasonings and the cooked onion and garlic until well combined.

Lay a large sheet of lightly greased aluminium foil on a flat surface. Lay the slices of pancetta slightly overlapping each other in a row down the middle of the aluminium foil. Place each chicken breast in a plastic bag and use a rolling pin to flatten out the breast. Lay the flattened breasts over the pancetta in one layer. Spread the minced meat mixture evenly over the breasts. Place the basil leaves over the meat and cover with the slices of ham. Lay the eggs in a long line down the centre on top of the ham.

Using the long edge of the aluminium foil roll up the roulade over the eggs to the opposite side, encasing the eggs in the roulade. Make sure the roll is enclosed by the aluminium foil. Twist the ends to seal. Place in a baking tray and cook in a preheated oven at 180°C for 1–1¼ hours. Cool, then unwrap and refrigerate.

When ready to serve, bring to room temperature and slice. Serve with a tasty relish or Pickled Red Cabbage (see recipe on page 81), salad or fresh rustic bread.

SERVES 12

from the earth

vegetables

Potato and Chicken Soup The restorative qualities of

chicken soup are well known. Thickened with Agria potatoes and

enriched with cream, this is a satisfying winter broth.

2 leeks, thinly sliced (white and edible green stem)

1 tablespoon olive oil

1 clove garlic, peeled and grated

2 teaspoons grated lemon zest

3 chicken thighs on the bone, skinned

4 large Agria potatoes, peeled and cut into small dice

2 cups water

4 cups chicken stock

1 bay leaf

sea salt and white pepper to taste

1 cup cream

½ cup fresh flat-leaf parsley, chopped

Thoroughly wash and drain the leeks before slicing. Place the leeks, olive oil and garlic in a saucepan and cook over a gentle heat for 5 minutes. Add the lemon zest, chicken thighs, diced potato, water, chicken stock and bay leaf. Cover with a lid and simmer gently for 20 minutes. Remove the chicken thighs, cut the meat from the bone into small pieces and return the meat to the soup. Season to taste. Simmer gently for a further 5 minutes. Just before serving, stir in the cream and chopped parsley.

SERVES 6

Potato and Chicken Soup

Zucchini and Broccolini Soup

1 small red onion, peeled and finely chopped

2 cloves garlic, peeled and grated

2 tablespoons olive oil

6 zucchini (courgettes), sliced

1½ cups blanched broccolini, chopped

sea salt and freshly ground black pepper to taste

4 cups chicken stock

2 cups water

1 cup cream

½ cup chopped fresh flat-leaf parsley

¼ cup grated parmesan cheese

extra grated parmesan cheese and parsley to garnish

Fry the onion and garlic in the olive oil over a gentle heat until soft. Add the zucchini and broccolini and allow them to sweat for 5 minutes. Season with salt and pepper. Add the chicken stock and water, cover, and simmer for 20 minutes. Cool and process in a blender. Return the soup to the saucepan, stir in the cream, parsley and parmesan cheese, and reheat. Serve in bowls, garnished with freshly ground black pepper, a little grated parmesan cheese and chopped parsley.

SERVES 6–8

Garlic Spinach

2 packed cups baby spinach leaves or torn regular leaves

2 large cloves garlic, peeled and grated

butter

extra virgin olive oil

sea salt and freshly ground black pepper to taste

fresh lemon juice

Wash, drain and dry the leaves well with absorbent kitchen paper. Fry the grated garlic with a knob of butter and a couple of tablespoons of extra virgin olive oil over a medium heat. Begin dropping in the greens a handful at a time, cooking them in three batches until they are wilted and tender. Season to taste with sea salt, ground black pepper and a squeeze of lemon juice.

SERVES 6

Spinach and Butternut Soup with Kumara Straws

Slightly bitter spinach leaves and sweet butternut combine to form a comforting and nourishing soup to satisfy you, especially during the cooler months. The crisp kumara straws add a satisfying finish.

1 leek (white part only), washed and sliced

2 tablespoons butter

1.5kg butternut, peeled and diced

1.5 litres bought or homemade chicken stock

2 bay leaves

sea salt and freshly ground black pepper to taste

2 packed cups baby spinach leaves

¼ cup cream

Place the leek and butter in a large saucepan and cook over a gentle heat until the leek softens. Add the butternut, chicken stock, bay leaves and seasonings. Cover and simmer gently until the butternut is just tender. Remove the bay leaves. Drop in the spinach leaves and simmer until they wilt. Just before serving, stir in the cream. Serve immediately, garnished with kumara straws.

SERVES 8

Kumara Straws

2 large golden kumara (sweet potato), peeled

oil for deep frying

Cut the kumara into 2–3mm-thick slices. Slice these into 2mm-wide straws. Deep-fry the straws in hot oil in batches until golden and crisp. Drain on absorbent kitchen paper, then sprinkle on top of the soup.

Eggplant with Parsley Sauce and Pomegranate

This is the easy way to experience the joy of pomegranates. The sweet but tart seeds in blush-pink juice are simply spooned over the crisp eggplant and parsley.

1 eggplant, cut into 1cm slices

¼ cup olive oil

2 cloves garlic, peeled

1 tightly packed cup fresh flat-leaf parsley

flaky sea salt to taste

½ cup pine nuts

¼ cup extra virgin olive oil

1 ripe pomegranate

Brush both sides of the eggplant slices with olive oil, then grill or barbecue on each side over a medium heat until tender and golden brown. Arrange on a serving plate.

Place the garlic, parsley, sea salt and pine nuts in a food processor and pulse until well chopped and combined. With the motor running, drizzle in the extra virgin olive oil to form a smooth paste. Spread a little parsley sauce over each eggplant slice. Cut the pomegranate in half and scoop out the seeds and juice. Sprinkle seeds and juice over the top of the eggplant.

SERVES 6

Eggplant with Parsley Sauce and Pomegranate

Roasted Asparagus When buying fresh asparagus, choose spears with firm, bright green stalks for maximum pleasure.

1 yellow pepper (capsicum), charred and skinned
1 red pepper (capsicum), charred and skinned
36 spears fresh asparagus
6 sprigs fresh thyme
6 thin slices prosciutto
25g butter
¼ cup extra virgin olive oil
1 cup good quality black olives
sea salt and freshly ground black pepper to taste
freshly grated nutmeg
juice of 1 lemon

Slice the flesh from the skinned peppers and set aside. Snap the ends from the asparagus, blanch the spears in boiling water, drain and dry on absorbent kitchen paper. Bundle together six asparagus spears and a sprig of thyme into six servings. Wrap each bundle around its middle with two slices of prosciutto. Place the bundles in a roasting pan with the butter and extra virgin olive oil. Sprinkle with the sliced pepper, olives, seasonings and nutmeg. Place in a preheated oven at 200°C and roast for 10 minutes or until the outer asparagus spears begin to brown, the butter goes nutty and the prosciutto is crispy. Remove from the oven and squeeze the lemon juice over. Serve immediately.

SERVES 6

Yams and Butternut Mash

800g golden yams

400g peeled butternut

1 tablespoon sea salt

1 bay leaf

$^{1}/_{2}$ cup cream

25g butter

sea salt and freshly ground black pepper to taste

Wash and drain the yams. Cut the butternut into small chunks. Place the vegetables in a saucepan with the salt, bay leaf and enough water to just cover the vegetables. Cook until tender. Drain and return to the saucepan. Add the cream, butter and seasonings to taste. Using a hand masher, work the ingredients to a creamy mash. Add extra butter if needed to achieve a smooth, thick mash. Taste and adjust seasonings if necessary.

SERVES 6

Potato and Kumara Gratin

500g Rua potatoes, peeled

500g golden kumara (sweet potato), peeled

1 cup milk

$1^{1}/_{2}$ cups cream

$^{1}/_{2}$ cup chopped fresh flat-leaf parsley

freshly grated nutmeg to taste

sea salt and freshly ground black pepper to taste

2 tablespoons butter

Thinly slice the potatoes and kumara and place in layers in a greased 2-litre capacity baking dish. Mix together the milk, cream, parsley, nutmeg and seasonings and pour over the vegetables. Dot the butter over the top. Bake in a preheated oven at 180°C for 1–1$^{1}/_{2}$ hours until the vegetables are tender and the top golden.

SERVES 6

Basil Grilled Vegetables You could serve this hot to accompany roast and grilled meats, or cold as a salad.

1 whole red pepper (capsicum)

1 whole yellow pepper (capsicum)

1 fennel root, thinly sliced

2 zucchini (courgettes), thinly sliced lengthways

1 eggplant (aubergine), sliced in rounds

16 asparagus spears, ends removed, blanched

2 cups fresh basil leaves

sea salt and freshly ground black pepper to taste

¼ cup extra virgin olive oil

1 tablespoon lemon juice

1 tablespoon red wine vinegar

1 clove garlic, peeled and grated

Place the peppers on a hot grill pan or barbecue to blister their skins. Set aside to cool while you cook the remaining vegetables. Grill the fennel, zucchini, eggplant and asparagus until slightly charred and tender. Remove the skins from the peppers and slice the flesh from the core, removing all the seeds. Place all the vegetables in a serving bowl with the fresh basil leaves. Season and add the extra virgin olive oil, lemon juice, red wine vinegar and garlic. Toss the ingredients together, taste and if necessary adjust the seasonings and dressing. Serve immediately.

SERVES 6

Roasted Parsnips and Carrots with Balsamic Vinegar and Parsley

4 medium carrots, peeled and cut into strips

3 small parsnips, peeled and cut into strips

extra virgin olive oil

sea salt and freshly ground black pepper to taste

¼ cup balsamic vinegar

⅓ cup chopped fresh flat-leaf parsley

Toss the carrots and parsnips in a bowl with enough extra virgin olive oil to coat the vegetables. Season with sea salt and black pepper. Spread them in a roasting pan in a single layer. Roast in a preheated oven at 180°C for 30 minutes, turning during cooking, until tender and slightly browned. Drain on absorbent kitchen paper and toss with the vinegar and parsley.

SERVES 6

Basil Grilled Vegetables

Beans with Parmesan Dressing

600g round or runner beans, thinly sliced, blanched, drained and dried

1 cup Niçoise black olives, stoned and chopped

½ cup sundried tomatoes, sliced

DRESSING

½ cup finely grated parmesan cheese

juice of 1 lemon

2 tablespoons lemon-infused extra virgin olive oil

1 tablespoon extra virgin olive oil

sea salt and freshly ground black pepper to taste

Place the beans, olives and sundried tomatoes in a bowl.

Mix together the parmesan cheese, lemon juice, lemon-infused extra virgin olive oil and extra virgin olive oil to make a runny dressing. Season with salt and black pepper. Use extra lemon juice or olive oil to adjust the flavour and taste.

Pile the beans onto a plate and drizzle with the dressing. Serve immediately.

SERVES 6

Chilli and Green Bean Stew

1 fresh red 'bird's eye' chilli, deseeded and finely chopped

3 cloves garlic, peeled and crushed

6 tablespoons olive oil

500g trimmed French beans or sliced flat beans

1 cup fresh flat-leaf parsley, finely chopped

½–¾ cup fresh dill, finely chopped

4–5 cups canned tomatoes in juice, finely chopped

sea salt and freshly ground black pepper to taste

pinch of sugar

Fry the chilli and garlic in the olive oil over a low heat until soft and aromatic. Add the beans and cook for a further 5 minutes. Stir in the herbs, tomatoes, salt, pepper and sugar. Simmer gently for 1 hour with the lid on, stirring occasionally. Serve warm or cold with grilled or roasted meats or on grilled bread as a snack.

SERVES 6

Pickled Walnut and Ebly Salad A soft, edible durum wheat, ebly is soaked to create a nutritious base for a unique savoury salad that can be eaten on its own, or served with grilled fish, poultry and meat.

1½ cups ebly

1 avocado, skinned, stoned and diced

3 spring onions, chopped

12 cherry tomatoes, halved

4 pickled walnuts, chopped coarsely

½ cup fresh flat-leaf parsley, chopped

grated zest of 1 lemon

juice of 1 lemon

sea salt and freshly ground black pepper to taste

avocado oil to moisten

Place the ebly in a bowl, cover with cold water and soak for 2 hours. Drain, dry on absorbent kitchen paper and place in a bowl. Add the avocado, spring onions, cherry tomatoes, pickled walnuts, parsley, lemon zest, lemon juice and seasonings. Gently toss together. Drizzle with the avocado oil and serve.

SERVES 6

Roasted Vegetables with Tomato and Rocket

200ml olive oil

3 cloves garlic, peeled and grated

250g butternut or pumpkin, peeled and diced

2 golden kumara (sweet potatoes), peeled and diced

1 large parsnip, peeled and diced

4 zucchini (courgettes), quartered

¼ cup fresh rosemary, crushed

¼ cup fresh sage leaves, chopped

sea salt and freshly ground black pepper to taste

½ cup fresh flat-leaf parsley, chopped

3 vine-ripened tomatoes, chopped

1 cup fresh rocket leaves

Place the olive oil, garlic, vegetables, rosemary, sage, salt and pepper into a bowl and toss them all together, ensuring the vegetables are well coated in oil. Place the vegetables in a baking pan and roast in a preheated oven at 180°C for 30 minutes or until soft. Cool slightly, then stir through the parsley, tomatoes and rocket leaves. Pile on a serving platter.

SERVES 6

Summer Salad Good-quality ingredients at their peak are essential to this salad. You can replace the rocket with greens of your choice. Fresh basil, mesclun or baby spinach also work well.

DRESSING

¼ **cup olive oil**

2 tablespoons lemon juice

2 tablespoons basil pesto (homemade or good quality bought)

1 tablespoon baby capers, washed and drained

rock salt to taste

SALAD

1 punnet (about 1½ cups) cherry tomatoes, halved

2 large tomatoes, coarsely chopped

½ **telegraph cucumber, peeled and sliced**

1 large avocado, peeled, stoned and chopped chunky

150g bocconcini, halved

2 cups rocket leaves

Process all the dressing ingredients in a blender. Place all the salad ingredients (except salad greens) in a large serving bowl. Pour the dressing over and toss gently. Place the salad greens on top and serve.

SERVES 6

Leek and Basil Lasagne

Leek and Basil Lasagne

BÉCHAMEL SAUCE

50g butter, melted

4 tablespoons plain flour

2$\frac{1}{2}$ cups milk

1 egg yolk

TOMATO SAUCE

1 onion, peeled and finely chopped

2 cloves garlic, peeled and grated

2 tablespoons olive oil

400g can tomatoes in juice, chopped

pinch of sugar

sea salt and freshly ground black pepper to taste

1 tablespoon balsamic vinegar

LEEKS

3 medium leeks, thinly sliced (white and edible green stem)

2 tablespoons butter

1 tablespoon olive oil

1 clove garlic, peeled and grated

$\frac{1}{2}$ cup chicken stock

sea salt and freshly ground black pepper to taste

ASSEMBLY

200g fresh lasagne sheets

1 cup fresh basil leaves

1$\frac{1}{4}$ cups ricotta cheese

1$\frac{1}{2}$ cups grated parmesan cheese

Make the Béchamel Sauce first. Melt the butter in a saucepan over a gentle heat. Stir in the flour to make a roux. Pour in one-third of the milk and stir until the sauce thickens. Add the remaining milk and whisk the sauce until smooth and thick. Cool slightly and whisk in the egg yolk.

Make the Tomato Sauce next. Cook the onion and garlic in the olive oil in a saucepan over a low heat until they soften. Add the tomatoes, sugar and seasonings. Simmer gently for 20 minutes. Stir in the balsamic vinegar. Cool, then purée.

Then prepare the leeks. Before slicing, thoroughly wash and drain the leeks. Place them in a saucepan with the butter, olive oil and garlic. Cook over a gentle heat for 5 minutes until the leeks soften. Add the chicken stock and seasonings and simmer gently until the liquid reduces and the green pieces of leek are still green but soft.

To assemble, butter a lasagne dish. Lay down a lasagne sheet to cover the bottom of the dish. Spread with half the Béchamel Sauce. Then spread half the Tomato Sauce on top. Evenly spread all the leeks over. Spoon the remaining Tomato Sauce over. Top all of this with another layer of lasagne. Scatter the basil leaves over. Pour and spread the remaining Béchamel Sauce over. Dot with all the ricotta and finally sprinkle with the parmesan cheese. Bake in a preheated oven at 180°C for 45 minutes.

SERVES 6–8

Onion, Herb and Tomato Crumble

olive oil for greasing

3 onions, peeled, halved and finely sliced

sea salt and freshly ground black pepper to taste

6 tomatoes, sliced

50g butter, cut into cubes

250g tasty vintage cheddar cheese, grated

$^1/_2$ cup chopped fresh basil and flat-leaf parsley, mixed together

2 slices stale white bread

2 tablespoons chopped fresh flat-leaf parsley, extra

2 tablespoons chopped fresh oregano leaves

Grease an 8-cup capacity deep pie dish with olive oil. Place half the sliced onions on the bottom of the pie dish. Season with salt and black pepper. Layer half the sliced tomatoes on top. Dot a third of the butter over the tomatoes. Sprinkle with half the cheese and fresh herbs. Repeat this process with the same quantity of ingredients and press down with your hand to compact. Pulse the bread and extra herbs in a processor to a fine crumb and sprinkle over the top. Dot with the remaining butter.

Bake in a preheated oven at 175°C for 1 hour or until all the ingredients are very soft, tender and melted. Leave at room temperature for 10 minutes before serving.

SERVES 6–8

Brunch Salad This style of salad is versatile and satisfying eaten for brunch, lunch or dinner. For a change, try replacing the bacon with smoked or wood-roasted salmon.

6 vine-ripened tomatoes, halved

2 tablespoons olive oil

sea salt and freshly ground black pepper to taste

pinch of sugar on each tomato half

2 cups ciabatta or French bread, crust removed, torn into
   bite-sized pieces

olive oil, extra, for cooking

6 cups crisp salad greens of your choice

12 slices streaky bacon, grilled and broken into pieces

6 fresh organic eggs, poached or soft-boiled

parmesan or pecorino cheese, in a piece

Place the tomato halves in a roasting pan and drizzle with the olive oil. Season, sugar and roast in a preheated oven at 180°C for 20 minutes until soft and juicy. Fry the bread in a little olive oil over a medium-high heat until golden, then drain on absorbent kitchen paper. Arrange the salad greens on six serving plates. Sprinkle with some bread and grilled bacon. Top with two roasted tomato halves per serve and a poached egg. Shave some parmesan or pecorino cheese over the top and drizzle with a little dressing.

DRESSING

1 egg yolk

½ cup olive oil

fresh lemon juice

sea salt to taste

¼ cup grated parmesan or pecorino cheese

Place the egg yolk in a bowl and with a whisk beat in the olive oil drop by drop until the dressing forms an emulsion and thickens. Continue to whisk in the olive oil in a slow, steady stream. Add enough fresh lemon juice to thin the dressing to the consistency of thick cream. Season to taste and stir in the parmesan cheese.

SERVES 6

Marinated Olive Salad

A selection of marinated olives are great pantry staples to have on hand during the summer, especially to make this tasty, fragrant brew.

2 cups green Greek olives

1¼ cups black Salvagno olives

1¼ cups black Taggiasca olives

¾ cup black Niçoise olives

julienned zest and juice of 1 lemon

4 fresh bay leaves

4 sprigs fresh thyme

2 large cloves garlic, peeled and thinly sliced

1 fresh red chilli, deseeded and diced

1 cup celery, finely chopped

¼ cup red wine vinegar

extra virgin olive oil

Combine all the ingredients in a large bowl, then pack into jars and top up with the extra virgin olive oil. Seal and refrigerate for 1–2 weeks to marinate. Serve as a separate salad to accompany a buffet meal or simply present in a bowl to snack on with evening drinks, or add to other salads as required.

This will keep in an airtight container in the fridge for up to 1 month.

SERVES 10–12

Marinated Olive Salad

Summer Salsa
The fresh ingredients in this recipe are the epitome of summer. It is a quick and easy accompaniment to prepare for serving alongside grilled and barbecued meats, fish and poultry or to spoon onto bruschetta.

4 firm vine-ripened tomatoes, skinned, quartered and deseeded
1 firm ripe avocado, halved, stoned and skinned
2 small fresh red 'bird's eye' chillies, deseeded and finely chopped
1 packed cup fresh coriander leaves, finely chopped
2 tablespoons chives, finely chopped
sea salt and freshly ground black pepper to taste
mayonnaise (see recipe for Lemon Mayonnaise on page 137)

Evenly dice the tomatoes and avocado and place in a bowl. Add the chillies, coriander, chives and seasonings to taste. Spoon in enough mayonnaise to bind the ingredients together.

MAKES 2 CUPS

Baby Beetroot

18 baby beetroot, washed (3–4 per person)

$^1/_4$ cup balsamic vinegar

1 bay leaf

1 teaspoon arrowroot

sea salt to taste

1 tablespoon fresh dill, chopped

Remove the tops from the beetroot but leave a small stem. Place the beets, vinegar, bay leaf and enough water to just cover the beets in a saucepan. Simmer gently until tender. Reserve $1^1/_2$ cups of liquid and drain off the remainder. Place the beets and reserved juices back in the saucepan. Mix the arrowroot to a paste with a little water and stir into the juices to thicken slightly. Season with salt to taste. Serve garnished with fresh dill.

SERVES 6

Pickled Red Cabbage

$^1/_2$ red cabbage

$^1/_4$ cup sea salt

300ml cider vinegar

300ml white wine vinegar

50ml balsamic vinegar

50ml water

4 tablespoons brown sugar

1 tablespoon coarsely ground black pepper

1 clove garlic, peeled and grated

1 teaspoon grated fresh ginger

1 teaspoon ground allspice

Remove the coarse outer cabbage leaves and cut the cabbage into quarters. Remove the core. With a sharp serrated knife, finely shred the cabbage, rinse under running water and drain. Place the cabbage in a large ceramic bowl or dish. Sprinkle with the sea salt and toss together. Cover with plastic food wrap and let it stand for 24 hours.

Transfer to a colander and drain. Place the vinegars, water, brown sugar, pepper, garlic, ginger and allspice in a saucepan and bring to the boil, then simmer gently for 5 minutes and set aside to cool. Dry the cabbage with absorbent kitchen paper and pack into sterilised jars. Pour the vinegar mixture over to cover the cabbage. Seal and store in a cool place for 1 week before eating. Once opened, store in the refrigerator for up to 3 weeks.

MAKES ABOUT 6 X 250G JARS

Mushroom and Bacon Pie

Mushroom and Bacon Pie

1¼ cups plain flour

¼ teaspoon sea salt

½ cup warm water

50g butter, melted

4 rashers thinly sliced middle bacon

3 tablespoons olive oil

1½ cups thinly sliced shiitake mushrooms

1½ cups thinly sliced portobello mushrooms

½ cup chopped fresh flat-leaf parsley

juice of ½ lemon or to taste

freshly ground black pepper to taste

½ cup grated parmesan cheese or another hard cheese

a little milk

Sift the flour into a bowl and add the salt. Make a well in the centre of the flour and, using a fork, mix in the warm water and the butter to form a dough. Turn onto a lightly floured board and knead until smooth. Wrap in plastic food wrap and chill for 30 minutes.

While the dough chills, fry the bacon in the olive oil over a medium heat for 5 minutes. Add the sliced mushrooms and cook for 10 minutes to soften, then stir in the parsley, lemon juice and black pepper. Set aside to cool.

Divide the dough in half and knead into two balls. On a lightly floured surface, roll half the dough into a rough circle about 26cm round, and place on a flat baking tray or pizza pan. Sprinkle with the cheese and the mushroom mixture, leaving a 5cm gap uncovered around the edge. Roll out the remaining dough to fit the top of the pie. Brush the uncovered base edge with milk, lay the lid on top, fold the base edges over the lid and flatten with a fork. Brush the top of the pie with milk and pierce at random with a fork. Bake in a preheated oven at 180°C for 35 minutes or until golden.

SERVES 10

Summer Picnic Bread

1 baguette

20 green olives, pitted and chopped

1/2 small red onion, peeled and finely diced

1 firm, ripe avocado, peeled, stoned and diced

juice of 1 lemon

6–8 vine-ripened tomatoes, deseeded and diced

6 anchovy fillets, drained and chopped

1 red pepper (capsicum), deseeded and finely diced

1/2 cup fresh flat-leaf parsley, chopped

1/2 cup fresh basil leaves

sea salt and freshly ground black pepper to taste

1/4 cup extra virgin olive oil

1 cup of these alternatives: crumbled feta or goat's cheese, sliced bocconcini, wood-roasted
  salmon or sliced hard-boiled eggs

Slice the baguette in half lengthways. Remove the bread from the inside of the baguette. Break it into small pieces and place in a bowl. Add to this the olives, onion, avocado, lemon juice, tomatoes, anchovies, pepper, parsley, basil, seasonings and enough of the extra virgin olive oil to moisten the ingredients. Spoon the mixture into the baguette shell and then top with a cup of your choice of alternatives. Place the other half of the baguette on top and press them together. Wrap in plastic food wrap and refrigerate overnight or until ready to tuck into your picnic pack.

SERVES 4

Cucumber and Mint Sandwiches

1 firm telegraph cucumber, peeled and thinly sliced

malt vinegar

250g cream cheese, softened

1 tablespoon lemon juice

sea salt and freshly ground black pepper to taste

20 slices brown sandwich bread

1/2 cup finely sliced fresh mint leaves

softened butter

Place the slices of cucumber in a shallow dish in a single layer and pour enough malt vinegar over to moisten all the cucumber. Leave to soak for 5 minutes. Drain the cucumber thoroughly on absorbent kitchen paper. Combine the softened cream cheese, lemon juice and seasonings to taste. Spread 10 slices of bread with the soft cream cheese mixture. Top the cream cheese with a layer of cucumber and then a sprinkling of fresh mint. Butter the remaining 10 slices of bread and place on top of each sandwich. Remove the crusts and cut each round into three fingers.

MAKES 30 FINGERS

from the dairy

eggs &
cheese

Scrambled Eggs with Peppers and Pancetta

Scrambled Eggs with Peppers and Pancetta

Soft, rich, creamy scrambled eggs pepped up with sweet peppers and crisp pancetta – a superb breakfast for guests. It's best to slightly undercook the eggs as they continue to cook when you remove them from the heat. Serve immediately.

PEPPERS

2 large red peppers (capsicums)

2 large yellow peppers (capsicums)

3 large, firm ripe tomatoes, blanched and skinned

4 tablespoons olive oil

sea salt and freshly ground black pepper to taste

pinch of paprika or to taste

pinch of sugar or to taste

EGGS

12 organic eggs

1/2 cup cream

1 tablespoon butter

12 slices pancetta (or streaky bacon), grilled crisp

Slice the flesh from the peppers and discard the core and seeds. Cut the peppers into strips. Cut the tomatoes into eighths and remove the seeds. Place the olive oil and peppers in a frying pan over a low to medium heat and cook for 10 minutes or until they soften. Add the tomatoes, seasonings and sugar and cover with a lid. Cook until the tomatoes soften.

Beat the eggs and cream together. Pour into a saucepan and add the butter. Cook over a low heat, stirring as the eggs coagulate, until they are soft and creamy. Serve the eggs and peppers with your favourite toast or grilled bread, with grilled pancetta.

SERVES 6

Savoury Eggs with Gazpacho Sauce

6 large organic eggs, hard-boiled

¼ cup homemade whole-egg mayonnaise (see recipe for Lemon
    Mayonnaise on page 137)

2 tablespoons avocado oil

sea salt and freshly ground black pepper to taste

2 tablespoons finely chopped semi-dried tomatoes

1 tablespoon finely chopped fresh basil

1 tablespoon finely chopped fresh chives

1 tablespoon finely chopped fresh flat-leaf parsley

1 tablespoon chopped toasted pine nuts

Shell the eggs and rinse them in cold water. Dry on absorbent kitchen paper and cut in half lengthways. Carefully remove the yolks, keeping the whites intact. Rinse the whites in cold water and drain on absorbent kitchen paper. Place the yolks, mayonnaise and avocado oil in a bowl and mash with a fork until smooth. Add the seasonings, semi-dried tomatoes, herbs and pine nuts and combine. Spoon equal amounts of the filling into the hollow in each egg.

Gazpacho Sauce

3 tomatoes, chopped

¼ telegraph cucumber, peeled, deseeded and chopped

½ red pepper (capsicum), deseeded and chopped

4 spring onions (white part only), chopped

1 clove garlic, peeled

¼ teaspoon paprika

1 cup white breadcrumbs

2 tablespoons sherry vinegar

¼ cup cold water

25ml extra virgin olive oil

Tabasco sauce to taste

sea salt and freshly ground black pepper to taste

rocket leaves

avocado oil

Place the tomatoes, cucumber, pepper, spring onions, garlic, paprika and breadcrumbs in a food processor and pulse until smooth. With the motor running, gradually pour in the vinegar, cold water, extra virgin olive oil and Tabasco sauce until well blended. Season to taste.

   Arrange the eggs on a serving platter or individual plates, surrounded with rocket leaves, a drizzle of Gazpacho Sauce and a drizzle of avocado oil.

SERVES 6

Cheese and Tomato Tart

400g bought puff pastry

butter for greasing

220g soft goat's cheese

$^{1}/_{2}$ cup fresh ricotta cheese

$^{1}/_{4}$ cup grated parmesan cheese

10–12 medium vine-ripened tomatoes

1$^{1}/_{2}$ cups fresh herbs (flat-leaf parsley, sage or basil),
  chopped

sea salt and freshly ground black pepper to taste

pinch of sugar

milk for brushing

2 tablespoons avocado oil

Roll out the pastry in a circle to fit a buttered 30cm loose-bottomed, fluted tart tin. Gently press the pastry into the tin. Prick the pastry all over with a fork. Refrigerate for 15 minutes or until the pastry firms.

Mix together both cheeses until well combined. Cut the tomatoes into slices. When the pastry is ready, spread the cheese mixture evenly over, leaving a 1cm border around the edge. Sprinkle with your choice of fresh herbs. Arrange the slices of tomato over the top of the filling, starting from the outside in overlapping circles finishing in the middle. Season to taste with salt, pepper and sugar. Brush the tart edge with a little milk. Bake in a preheated oven at 200°C for 40 minutes or until the pastry is puffed, cooked and golden around the edge. Drizzle with the avocado oil and serve warm.

SERVES 6

Cheese and Tomato Tart

Parsley and Feta Dip
A fresh, slightly peppery-flavoured dip that takes little time to prepare.

2 packed cups fresh flat-leaf parsley

150g feta cheese, crumbled

2 spring onions, chopped

1 clove garlic, peeled

2 tablespoons lemon juice

¼ cup extra virgin olive oil

sea salt to taste

extra 50g feta cheese, crumbled

Place the parsley, feta, spring onions, garlic and lemon juice in a food processor and pulse to chop the mixture. With the motor running, drizzle in the extra virgin olive oil until you have a smooth, thick paste. Add extra oil if you need to. Stir in the extra crumbled feta and serve with Grilled Flat Bread (see recipe below).

MAKES 1 CUP

Grilled Flat Bread

30g dried yeast

½ cup warm water

500g plain flour

pinch of salt

50g butter, softened

2 teaspoons olive oil

warm water, extra

Dissolve the yeast in the warm water. Cover the bowl and allow the mixture to become frothy (about 15 minutes). Place the flour and salt in another bowl and mix together. When the yeast froths, pour it into the flour along with the butter, olive oil and enough extra warm water to form a ball of soft dough. Knead for 10 minutes then cover and leave to rise for 1 hour until double its size.

To cook the bread, heat a chargrill or ribbed pan over a moderate heat. Take pieces of dough and roll them out on a floured board into 16 rounds about 5mm thick. Brush the grill or pan with a little olive oil and cook the rounds for 1–2 minutes on each side and serve with your favourite dip or pâté.

MAKES 16

Parsley and Feta Dip

Baked Ricotta with Goat's Cheese and Herbs

Mild, soft ricotta spiked with goat's cheese and baked. What could be easier for a moreish snack to serve with drinks?

400g fresh ricotta cheese
120g creamy goat's cheese
1 egg yolk
1 tablespoon fresh basil, chopped
1 tablespoon fresh flat-leaf parsley, chopped
1 tablespoon fresh chives, chopped
sea salt and freshly ground black pepper to taste
extra virgin olive oil for greasing and serving

Combine the ricotta, goat's cheese, egg yolk, basil, parsley, chives and seasonings. Spoon into 4 greased ½ cup-capacity ovenproof ramekins. Bake in a preheated oven at 160°C for 30 minutes until set. Alternatively, use 1 greased 2½ cup-capacity dish and bake for 45 minutes.

Cool slightly, then remove from the ramekins and place on a baking tray. Pat dry with absorbent kitchen paper, brush with a little extra virgin olive oil and place under a hot grill to brown. Transfer to a serving plate and drizzle with a tablespoon of extra virgin olive oil. Serve with a little Summer Salsa (see recipe on page 80) on the side for a light lunch or with crisp breads and drinks.

MAKES 4 SMALL CHEESES OR 1 LARGE CHEESE

Baked Ricotta with Goat's Cheese and Herbs

Feta, Rocket and Rock Melon Salad

Try this combination of creamy feta, peppery rocket and juicy rock melon for a refreshing summer salad.

1 rock melon, halved, deseeded, peeled and sliced
300g cow's milk feta cheese, sliced or crumbled
1 red onion, peeled, halved and thinly sliced
2 packed cups rocket leaves
1/4 cup avocado oil
2 tablespoons lemon juice
freshly ground black pepper to taste

Divide the rock melon slices among six plates and top with feta, onion and rocket leaves. Drizzle with the avocado oil and lemon juice and season to taste with black pepper.

SERVES 6

Watercress and Tomato Salad

6 vine-ripened tomatoes, quartered
2 cups cherry tomatoes, halved
3/4 cup semi-dried tomatoes
2 packed cups fresh watercress leaves
1/3 cup extra virgin olive oil
1 clove garlic, peeled and grated
2 tablespoons red wine vinegar
sea salt and freshly ground black pepper to taste

Place the tomatoes and watercress in a bowl and toss together to combine. Place the extra virgin olive oil, garlic, vinegar and seasonings in a jar and shake together to combine. Just before serving, drizzle the dressing over the salad.

SERVES 6

Feta, Rocket and Rock Melon Salad

Cheese and Chilli Pizza This combination of tasty, rich and creamy cheeses, spiked with chilli, and lightly sweetened red peppers and honey, is perfect to offer friends at a long lazy weekend lunch.

CHILLI TOMATO SAUCE

2 tablespoons olive oil

2 cloves garlic, peeled and chopped

1 large onion, peeled and finely chopped

4 x 400g cans tomatoes in juice

sea salt and cracked black pepper to taste

½ teaspoon sugar

1 bay leaf

DOUGH

¼ cup warm water

2 teaspoons dried yeast

pinch of sugar

1 cup warm water

3 tablespoons olive oil

pinch of sea salt

2¾ cups plain flour

TOPPING

2 large red peppers (capsicums)

olive oil for grilling

2 cups Chilli Tomato Sauce

2 tablespoons liquid honey

200g feta cheese, crumbled

200g haloumi cheese, grated

200g mozzarella cheese, sliced

fresh rocket leaves

plain yoghurt

Make the sauce first. In a large saucepan, heat the olive oil and fry the garlic and onion over a low heat until soft. Add the tomatoes, seasonings, sugar and bay leaf and simmer gently for 20 minutes. Allow to cool, remove the bay leaf and mash or purée the sauce.

To make the dough, place the first measure of warm water in a bowl and sprinkle the yeast and sugar over. Leave in a warm place until the mixture bubbles and becomes foamy. Add the second measure of warm water, the olive oil, salt and flour, and mix together until it forms a dough. Transfer the dough to a lightly floured board. Knead until the dough is shiny, smooth and elastic. This should take 5–10 minutes. Place the dough in a lightly oiled bowl and cover with plastic food wrap. Put the bowl in a warm place and allow the dough to rise until double its size. This should take 1–1½ hours.

Knock down the dough and knead it into a smooth ball ready to use. Divide the dough in half and roll out on a lightly floured board to make two pizza rounds. Spread with sauce and topping as described below.

To make the topping, brush the red peppers with olive oil and grill under a medium-high heat until they blister. Cool and peel. Spread each pizza base with 1 cup of Chilli Tomato Sauce. Arrange the peppers over the top. Drizzle with a little liquid honey. Sprinkle the cheeses over and bake in a preheated oven at 220°C for 15–20 minutes. Top with rocket leaves and drizzle with a little runny yoghurt. Serve warm.

SERVES 12

Mozzarella and Tomato Melt   A simple, yet deliciously savoury assembly of good-quality summer tastes for lunch.

butter, softened

fresh white sandwich-sliced bread

buffalo mozzarella cheese, thinly sliced

fresh basil leaves

vine-ripened tomatoes

olive oil

Butter both sides of the bread slices. Place them on a flat surface. Place slices of mozzarella over the surface of the bread, top with a layer of fresh basil leaves and slices of vine-ripened tomato. Top with a remaining bread slice.

Melt a knob of butter and olive oil in the bottom of a non-stick frying pan. Once the butter sizzles, carefully place the sandwich in the pan and fry for 2–3 minutes each side or until golden and the cheese is melted. Serve warm. Alternatively, use an electric sandwich maker.

Brown and White Fudge Brownies This is a

gorgeously rich, moist and dense brownie, ideal for serving with coffee or

with berries as dessert. It's easiest to make two separate mixtures, and then

work with both when assembling the brownie prior to baking.

2 x 60g butter
100g dark chocolate, chopped
2 x 100g sugar
2 x 1 teaspoon vanilla extract
2 x ¼ cup mascarpone
2 x 1 egg
2 x 100g plain flour, sifted
100g white chocolate, chopped

Place the first measure of butter and dark chocolate in a heatproof bowl and melt over a pot of barely simmering water or in the microwave on low power. While the chocolate melts, beat together the first measures of sugar, vanilla, mascarpone and egg until well combined. Stir in the melted chocolate mixture, followed by the first measure of flour, until well combined. Set aside.

Repeat this process with the second measure of ingredients, this time using the white chocolate, so that you have two separate bowls of mixture – one with dark chocolate and the other with white. Drop spoonfuls of both mixtures randomly into a 20-cm buttered square cake tin. Loosely swirl the mixtures into each other with a wooden skewer. Bake in a preheated oven at 170–180°C for 30–35 minutes or until firm. Cool in the tin before cutting.

MAKES 20

Cappuccino Cream Cake

CAKE

butter for greasing

150g ground almonds

3 tablespoons caster sugar

2 tablespoons cornflour

5 egg whites

150g caster sugar

Cut 3 x 20cm circles of baking paper and grease. Combine the ground almonds, caster sugar and cornflour and set aside. Beat the egg whites until they form stiff peaks and gradually add the second measure of caster sugar, beating until the mixture is very thick, smooth and shiny. Fold in the ground almond mixture.

Divide the mixture between the circles of baking paper and spread it evenly. Bake in a preheated oven at 180°C for about 25 minutes or until the layers are slightly crisp. Loosen each cake from its paper and turn onto a cake cooler. Remove the paper lining from the bottom of each cake layer.

CAPPUCCINO PASTRY CREAM

6 egg yolks

125g caster sugar

50g plain flour, sifted

500ml milk

1 tablespoon double-strength cold black coffee

1 cup toasted almond flakes

Beat the egg yolks with the caster sugar and flour until smooth, then strain through a sieve. Place the milk and coffee in a saucepan and bring to the boil. Remove from the heat and whisk in the sieved mixture. Return the mixture to a low heat and stir constantly until the pastry cream thickens. Pour into a bowl, cool, cover and refrigerate to thoroughly chill.

To assemble, place a layer of cake on a serving plate. Spread about one-third of the pastry cream evenly over the cake. Repeat this process with each layer of cake. Allow enough pastry cream to cover the top and sides of the cake. Sprinkle the top and sides of the cake liberally with toasted almond flakes.

SERVES 8–10

from the orchard

Apricotta Cake
Almond-flavoured amaretti biscuits form the base of this rustic baked ricotta cheesecake. Its richness is tempered by the apricots.

100g amaretti biscuits, crushed
150g plain sweet biscuits, crushed
100g butter, melted
12 fresh apricots, halved and stoned
400g ricotta cheese
400g mascarpone
3 eggs
1 cup caster sugar
1 tablespoon brandy

Stir together the crushed biscuits and melted butter, and press into the bottom of a 23cm springform cake tin. Arrange the apricot halves cut-side down over the base. Place the ricotta, mascarpone, eggs, caster sugar and brandy in a food processor and pulse until the mixture is smooth. Pour the ricotta mixture over the apricots and base. Bake in a preheated oven at 150°C for 1 hour. Remove from the oven and cool in the tin before removing. Serve with a drizzle of Caramel Sauce.

SERVES 8–10

Caramel Sauce

⅓ cup water
⅔ cup sugar
4 tablespoons cream

Stir together the water and sugar in a saucepan over a low heat until the sugar dissolves. Increase the heat and simmer the syrup gently until it caramelises. Remove from the heat and, when it stops bubbling, stir in the cream.

MAKES 1 CUP

Apricotta Cake

Quince Tart
Soft, fragrant stewed quinces mingle with cinnamon, honey and crunchy nuts in a tantalising tart.

4 large quinces, peeled, cored and sliced

1 cup sugar

$^3/_4$ cup water

2 slices lemon peel

3 tablespoons butter, melted

6 sheets filo pastry

$^1/_2$ cup blanched almonds, chopped

1 teaspoon cinnamon

2 tablespoons runny honey

1 tablespoon caster sugar

Place the quinces, sugar, water and lemon peel in a large saucepan and simmer for 20–30 minutes until the quinces are tender and pink. Set aside to cool. Grease a 23cm ceramic pie plate with butter. Line the pie plate with four sheets of filo pastry, brushing the melted butter in between the layers. Allow the excess pastry to flop over the edge. Sprinkle the almonds over the bottom of the lined pie dish and shake the cinnamon over. Drizzle with the honey and pile the quinces in. Lay the extra sheets of filo pastry over, buttered between the layers as before. Fold the excess pastry from the edges over and butter them down. Sprinkle with the caster sugar. Bake in a preheated oven at 160°C for 30 minutes or until golden and crisp. Serve warm with ice-cream or cream.

SERVES 6

Lemon Syrup Cake

125g butter, softened

2 teaspoons grated lemon zest

1 cup caster sugar

4 eggs

2 cups ground almonds

1 cup self-raising flour

¼ cup lemon juice

¾ cup caster sugar, extra

Cream the butter, lemon zest and caster sugar together until pale. Add the eggs one at a time, beating well after each addition. Stir in the ground almonds and flour. Spoon the mixture into a well-buttered cake tin, any shape as long as it is the equivalent capacity of a 20cm cake tin. Bake at 180°C for 40 minutes or until an inserted skewer comes out clean.

Cool for 5 minutes, then invert the cake onto a serving plate. Stir the lemon juice and extra measure of caster sugar together and pour over the cake.

SERVES 8

Feijoa Panacotta

4 feijoas, peeled

lemon juice

2 tablespoons caster sugar

650ml cream

6 tablespoons caster sugar, extra

2 teaspoons gelatine

fresh feijoas, extra, peeled and sliced

Coarsely chop the feijoas and place in a bowl, then squeeze some lemon juice over to help prevent browning. Add the first measure of caster sugar. Place in the microwave and cook on high for 1 minute or until the sugar dissolves. Cool and purée.

Place the cream and extra caster sugar in a saucepan and stir over a gentle heat until the sugar dissolves. Remove from the heat and sprinkle the gelatine over. Return to the heat and stir in until the gelatine completely dissolves. Remove from the heat, cool slightly and stir in the puréed feijoa. Pour the mixture into six dariole moulds or ramekins. Cover with plastic food wrap and refrigerate until set.

To unmould the panacotta, run a sharp knife around the top of the mould and invert onto a serving plate. Serve immediately with fresh sliced feijoas on the side.

SERVES 6

Peach and Chocolate Tart

I like to make this tart when white-skinned peaches are available. Canned peach halves could also be used to make an out-of-season treat.

PASTRY

2 cups plain flour

1 cup icing sugar, sifted

100g chilled butter, cubed

1 egg

1–2 tablespoons cold water

FILLING

5 fresh peaches, blanched and skinned

2 tablespoons butter, softened

$\frac{1}{2}$ cup brown sugar

3 eggs, beaten

100g dark chocolate, melted

CHOCOLATE SAUCE

100g dark chocolate

2 tablespoons cream

Place the flour, icing sugar and butter in a food processor and pulse the mixture to resemble fine breadcrumbs. Add the egg and enough water to process the mixture to form a ball of dough. Wrap in plastic food wrap and refrigerate for 30 minutes. When ready to use, roll out the pastry onto a lightly floured board, ensuring the pastry is large enough to fit a 23cm loose-bottomed, fluted tart tin. Line the base with baking paper and fill with pie beans to bake blind in a preheated oven at 180°C for 10–15 minutes until firm and golden. Cool and remove the paper and pie beans. Set aside while you prepare the filling.

Halve the peaches and remove the stones. Place the peaches cut-side down over the bottom of the tart base. Cream together the butter and brown sugar until light and pale. Beat in the eggs and chocolate, then pour the mixture over the peaches. Bake in a preheated oven at 180°C for 30–35 minutes. Cool, then remove from the tin.

To make the chocolate sauce, melt together the chocolate and cream in the microwave on low. Serve the tart at room temperature with a drizzle of chocolate sauce on the side.

SERVES 8

Peach and Chocolate Tart

Cherry Pies

butter for greasing

750g bought or homemade sweet short-crust pastry

600g fresh cherries, stoned

⅓ cup caster sugar

¼ cup fresh orange juice

milk for glazing

icing sugar for serving

mascarpone for serving

Butter six 10cm fluted, loose-bottomed aluminium pie cases. Roll out two-thirds of the pastry and cut six 12cm circles. Ease the circles into the pie cases and allow the extra pastry to lap over the top. Roll out the remaining pastry and cut out six 10cm circles for the pie tops. Lay the pie tops flat on a plate lined with baking paper and place in the fridge along with the lined pastry cases while you prepare the filling.

Place the cherries, caster sugar and orange juice in a saucepan over a gentle heat and stir together until the sugar dissolves, then cool.

To assemble the pies, spoon the cherry filling into the pie cases. Brush the overlapping pastry with a little milk and place the tops on. Seal the edges and trim off the excess pastry. Brush the tops with a little milk and pierce each one a couple of times with a fork. Bake in a preheated oven at 200°C for 20–25 minutes until cooked and golden. Remove from the oven and allow to cool. When the pies are cool, remove them from their cases. Dredge the tops with a little icing sugar and serve with a dollop of mascarpone.

SERVES 6

Cherry Pies

Blackberry Meringue Pudding

PUDDING BOTTOM

butter for greasing

12 Italian sponge fingers, crumbled

3 eggs yolks (save the whites for the top)

$^3/_4$ cup milk

$^3/_4$ cup cream

$^3/_4$ cup mascarpone

3 tablespoons caster sugar

FILLING

$2^1/_2$ cups blackberries

1 tablespoon fresh orange juice

2 tablespoons caster sugar

MERINGUE TOPPING

3 egg whites

6 tablespoons caster sugar

Butter six 200ml ramekins. Spoon the sponge finger crumbs evenly into the ramekins. Beat together the egg yolks, milk, cream, mascarpone and caster sugar. Pour the egg yolk mixture over the crumbs. Bake in a preheated oven at 150°C for 20–25 minutes until set. Remove from the oven and cool.

While the bases cool place the blackberries, orange juice and caster sugar in a saucepan, bring to a gentle boil and stir until the sugar dissolves. Remove from the heat and spoon the filling over the cooked base.

For the meringue topping, beat the egg whites until stiff, then gradually beat in the caster sugar. Dollop the meringue on top of the ramekins. Bake in a preheated oven at 200°C for 10–15 minutes until the meringue is set and golden.

SERVES 6

Blackberry Meringue Pudding

Cherry Swirls
An impressive-looking biscuit, made with a simple almond-spiked dough and sweet cherry paste. They will keep in an airtight container for about five days.

DOUGH

250g butter, softened

³/₄ cup sugar

1 teaspoon almond essence

1 egg yolk

2¹/₄ cups plain flour

¹/₂ cup ground almonds

FILLING

¹/₂ cup blanched almonds

³/₄ cup glacé cherries

¹/₂ cup mixed peel

¹/₄ cup apricot jam

To make the dough, beat together the butter and sugar until pale and creamy. Add the almond essence and egg yolk and beat until combined. Beat in the flour and ground almonds to form a firm, smooth dough. Line a 36 x 25cm baking pan with non-stick baking paper and press the dough evenly into the pan and smooth the surface. Refrigerate for 30 minutes to firm while you make the filling.

To make the filling, place the blanched almonds in a food processor and pulse to finely grind. Add the glacé cherries and mixed peel, and process to a paste. Add the apricot jam and pulse to combine.

To assemble, remove the firm dough from the baking pan and place on a flat surface. Spread with the filling. Roll up the cookie dough lengthways into a tight log shape. Wrap in baking paper and refrigerate until firm. When ready to cook, remove from the fridge and, using a serrated knife, cut 5mm rounds and place on a non-stick baking tray, well spaced. Bake in a preheated oven at 180°C for 15–20 minutes or until light golden.

MAKES 20

Lemon and Honey Nut Tart
Sweet, sour and crunchy, this Italian-influenced tart benefits from the unique flavour of manuka honey.

BASE

160g butter, softened

$^3/_4$ cup caster sugar

2 large eggs

$^3/_4$ cup plain flour

1 cup ground almonds

FILLING

250g butter

$^1/_2$ cup caster sugar

3 eggs

$^1/_2$ cup manuka honey, melted

$^1/_2$ teaspoon pure vanilla extract

1 teaspoon grated lemon zest

$^3/_4$ cup fresh walnuts, coarsely chopped

$^3/_4$ cup lightly toasted pine nuts

1 cup plain flour

SAUCE

$^1/_4$ cup manuka honey, melted

2 tablespoons fresh lemon juice

To make the base, cream the butter and caster sugar until pale and fluffy. Beat in the eggs, one at a time. Add the flour and ground almonds and stir together to combine. Spoon the mixture into a 25–30cm greased loose-bottomed tart flan and, using your hands, spread the mixture evenly over the base. Prick the base all over and bake in a preheated oven at 180°C for 10 minutes.

While the base cooks, prepare the filling. Beat together the butter and caster sugar until pale and fluffy. Beat in the eggs, one at a time. Stir in the honey, vanilla extract, lemon zest, walnuts, pine nuts and flour. Spoon over the cooked tart base and bake at 170°C for about 30 minutes or until the mixture has just set. Cool.

Melt together the extra honey and lemon juice for the sauce. Serve the tart at room temperature with a little whipped cream and a drizzle of sauce.

SERVES 6–8

Pears Caramelised on Almond Shortcake

SHORTCAKE

100g butter, softened

$^{1}/_{2}$ cup caster sugar

$^{3}/_{4}$ cup ground almonds

$^{3}/_{4}$ cup plain flour

CARAMELISED TOPPING

250g mascarpone

2 tablespoons icing sugar

$^{1}/_{2}$ teaspoon pure vanilla extract

2 tablespoons butter

4–5 pears, peeled, cored and quartered

$^{1}/_{2}$ cup caster sugar

1 tablespoon lemon juice

1 tablespoon grated lemon zest

Cream the butter and caster sugar together until pale. Stir in the ground almonds and flour. Press the dough evenly into an oblong tart tin (about 34 x 10cm or round equivalent) and prick it all over with a fork. Bake in a preheated oven at 150°C for 15–20 minutes until cooked but still pale. Remove from the oven and cool.

Combine the mascarpone, icing sugar and vanilla extract. Spread this evenly over the cooled base and refrigerate. Melt the butter over a medium heat and add the pears and caster sugar. Cook over a medium heat until the pears are tender and the juices have caramelised. Add the lemon juice and zest. Cool, then, when ready to serve, spoon the fruit and juices over the mascarpone and almond shortcake base. To serve, cut into slices and drizzle with a little crème anglaise.

SERVES 6–8

Pears Caramelised on Almond Shortcake

Baked Tamarillos with Walnut Iced Cream

Tart and tangy tamarillos are a perfect foil for the Walnut Iced Cream.

6 firm, ripe tamarillos

3 tablespoons sugar

$^1/_2$ teaspoon pure vanilla extract

2 tablespoons brandy

$^1/_2$ cup orange juice

WALNUT ICED CREAM

3 egg yolks

$^1/_2$ cup caster sugar

2 tablespoons brandy

300ml cream, whipped thick

200g mascarpone

1 cup fresh walnuts, chopped coarsely

To prepare the tamarillos, slice the stalks from the tamarillos. Using a sharp vegetable peeler or knife, remove the skins from the tamarillos. Cut the fruit in half lengthways. Place the tamarillos cut-side down in a baking dish just large enough to fit the fruit. Sprinkle with the sugar.

Stir together the vanilla extract, brandy and orange juice, then pour over the fruit. Cover with aluminium foil and bake in a preheated oven at 200°C for 10 minutes. Turn the fruit and bake for a further 10 minutes. Spoon into a serving bowl, cool and chill in the fridge. Bring to room temperature 1 hour before serving. Serve with a scoop of Walnut Iced Cream.

To make the Walnut Iced Cream, beat the egg yolks, caster sugar and brandy together until thick and pale. Using another bowl, fold together the whipped cream and mascarpone. Add the cream and walnuts to the egg mixture and fold together. Pour into a suitable container for freezing. Cover with aluminium foil and freeze overnight.

SERVES 6

Baked Tamarillos with Walnut Iced Cream

Strawberries and Mint When

strawberries are in season, this makes a quick,

refreshing, sweet finish to any meal, which is

easily prepared and can be ready in moments.

4 cups strawberries, hulled and halved
$1/4$ cup caster sugar
2 tablespoons freshly chopped mint leaves
250g mascarpone
2 tablespoons caster sugar, extra

Place the strawberries in a serving bowl. Process the
caster sugar and chopped mint in a processor.
Sprinkle the sugar and mint over the strawberries
and gently toss together. Mix together the
mascarpone and caster sugar, spoon a little into a
serving bowl (glass looks fantastic) and top with the
minted strawberries.

SERVES 6

Strawberries and Mint

Blackberry Tart
Supremely quick, simple and easy to assemble when you need an impressive pudding in a hurry. Any other berry could be substituted with equally delicious results.

2 sheets bought puff pastry, 23 x 24cm

1 egg white, lightly beaten

2 tablespoons caster sugar

500g crème fraîche

4 cups fresh blackberries

2 tablespoons vanilla sugar (see recipe on page 136)

To form the base, lace one sheet of pastry on a greased baking tray. From the second sheet of pastry, cut eight 1cm-wide strips. Brush the base with egg white. Place half the strips around the edge to form a border. Brush the border with egg white and place the remaining strips on top of the existing border. Prick the base all over with a fork. Sprinkle the base and edge with caster sugar. Cover with plastic wrap and chill in the fridge for 30 minutes.

Bake the base in a preheated oven at 200°C for 15 minutes or until golden and crisp. Cool.

To serve, spread the pastry with crème fraîche. Squash the blackberries with a fork and sprinkle with the vanilla sugar. Spoon the blackberries over the pastry and crème fraîche.

SERVES 6

Blackberry Tart

Tropical Torte

BASE

3/4 cup pistachio nuts

1/2 cup desiccated coconut

1/2 cup icing sugar

4 egg whites

1/2 cup caster sugar

Process the pistachios in a food processor until finely ground. Combine the ground pistachios in a bowl with the coconut and icing sugar. Beat the egg whites until stiff, then gradually add the caster sugar until it dissolves and the meringue is thick, shiny and stiff. Fold the pistachio mixture through the meringue. Spread the mixture in a 25cm loose-bottomed cake tin lined with baking paper and smooth the top. Bake in a preheated oven at 160°C for 25 minutes or until just firm. Completely cool, then transfer carefully to a serving plate.

TOPPING

1 egg white

2 tablespoons caster sugar

300g mascarpone

1/2 teaspoon pure vanilla extract

2 fresh passionfruit

1 kiwifruit, peeled and sliced

1/2 mango, peeled and sliced

1/4 cup fresh pineapple, peeled, cored and sliced

1/8 fresh honey dew melon, peeled and sliced

1/8 fresh rock melon, peeled and sliced

Beat the egg white until stiff, then gradually beat in the caster sugar until dissolved. Combine the mascarpone, vanilla extract, and the pulp from the passionfruit. Gently fold the beaten egg white through the mascarpone mixture. Cover and refrigerate for 2 hours. One hour before serving, spread the passionfruit mascarpone over the torte base and return to the fridge. When ready to serve, arrange the sliced fruit randomly over the top of the torte.

SERVES 6–8

Fig and Gingernut Fingers

BASE

250g packet gingernut biscuits

$^1/_2$ cup walnuts, finely chopped

$^1/_2$ cup finely chopped dried figs

1 teaspoon ground ginger

100g butter

$^1/_4$ cup bought or homemade caramelised sweetened condensed milk

$^1/_4$ cup brown sugar

ICING

1$^1/_2$ cups icing sugar

$^1/_2$ teaspoon ground ginger

1 tablespoon melted butter

1 teaspoon grated orange zest

2 tablespoons orange juice

$^1/_4$ cup crystallised ginger, sliced

Crush the gingernuts to fine crumbs using a rolling pin or food processor and place in a bowl with the chopped walnuts, figs and ground ginger. Stir together. Melt together the butter and caramelised condensed milk. Add the brown sugar and dissolve over a low heat. Add the melted ingredients to the biscuit crumb mixture and combine well. Press the mixture firmly into a shallow baking pan about 26 x 22cm.

For the icing, sift the icing sugar and ground ginger into a bowl. Add the melted butter, orange zest and orange juice. Beat together until smooth and spread evenly over the slice. Sprinkle the sliced crystallised ginger over the top. Refrigerate until firm, then cut into fingers.

MAKES 30

Rich Christmas Cake
A rich, no-fuss Christmas cake, this really is easy to prepare despite the long list of ingredients.

$^3/_4$ cup sultanas

1 cup raisins

1 cup currants

$^1/_2$ cup pitted prunes, chopped

$^1/_2$ cup pitted dates, chopped

$^1/_2$ cup dried figs, chopped

$^1/_2$ cup mixed peel

$^1/_2$ cup glacé cherries

2 tablespoons apricot jam

$^1/_2$ cup dark cream sherry

1 tablespoon each grated lemon zest and juice

1 tablespoon each grated orange zest and juice

butter for greasing

100g butter, chopped and softened

$^3/_4$ cup brown sugar, firmly packed

3 eggs

75g dark chocolate, grated

$^1/_2$ cup pecan nuts, chopped

$^1/_4$ cup whole brazil nuts

1 cup plain flour, sifted

$^1/_2$ cup self-raising flour, sifted

2 tablespoons Dutch cocoa powder, sifted

TO FINISH

whole pecan nuts to decorate the top

$^1/_4$ cup apricot jam

1 tablespoon sherry

The Night Before
Place all the dried fruit, apricot jam, sherry, zest and juices in a large bowl and stir together. Cover and marinate overnight or longer. Line a 23cm cake tin with two layers of brown paper and a layer of baking paper greased with butter.

The Next Day
Cream the butter and brown sugar together until pale. Add the eggs, one at a time, beating well after each addition. Stir in the chocolate, nuts, sifted dry ingredients and marinated fruit until very well combined. Spoon the mixture into the prepared cake tin and spread evenly.

Decorate the top with circles of pecan nuts. Bake in a preheated oven at 150°C for about 3 hours. While the cake is still warm, melt the apricot jam and sherry together in a saucepan over a low heat. Put through a sieve and then brush over the nuts on top of the cake to glaze.

SERVES 10–12

Raspberry Semifreddo with Raspberry Ice

2 eggs, separated

³/₄ cup caster sugar

600ml cream, whipped

3 cups fresh raspberries, coarsely mashed

1 tablespoon cassis (blackcurrant) liqueur

Beat the egg yolks with ¹/₄ cup of the caster sugar until pale. Fold the egg yolks and sugar into the cream until well combined. Beat the egg whites until stiff, then gradually beat in the remaining caster sugar until stiff and glossy and fold into the cream mixture. Fold the raspberries and cassis through this mixture. Pour into 12 x 150ml ramekins, cover with aluminium foil and place in the freezer overnight or for 4 hours until frozen.

To remove the semifreddo from the ramekins, leave sitting at room temperature for 5 minutes. Run a knife around the top edge of the ramekins and turn onto a serving plate. Serve with Raspberry Ice spooned on top.

Raspberry Ice Make this just before serving.

1¹/₂ cups frozen raspberries

¹/₄ cup caster sugar

Place the frozen raspberries and caster sugar in a blender or food processor and whiz them together so they are still chunky and icy for serving. Spoon on top of the semifreddo.

SERVES 12

Raspberry Semifreddo with Raspberry Ice

Rhubarb and Apple Hazelnut Puddings

Rhubarb and Apple Hazelnut Puddings

700g rhubarb

$^1/_2$ **cup water**

$^1/_2$ **cup caster sugar**

1 strip lemon rind

1 cup stewed apple

butter for greasing

2 eggs

$^1/_3$ **cup sugar**

1 teaspoon lemon juice

1 teaspoon grated lemon zest

$^1/_2$ **cup self-raising flour, sifted**

$^1/_4$ **teaspoon freshly grated nutmeg, sifted**

$^1/_4$ **cup cornflour, sifted**

$^1/_2$ **teaspoon baking powder, sifted**

$^1/_2$ **cup ground hazelnuts**

icing sugar

Remove the strings and leafy ends from the rhubarb and cut the stalks into chunks. Place the rhubarb, water, caster sugar and lemon strip in a saucepan with the lid on and simmer gently over a medium heat until the fruit is just soft. Cool, then stir in the stewed apple. Butter six 200ml ramekins. Beat the eggs and sugar together until thick and pale. Add the lemon juice and zest, and the sifted flour, nutmeg, cornflour, baking powder and ground hazelnuts and fold together. Put an equal amount of fruit into each ramekin. Spoon the batter over the fruit. Bake in a preheated oven at 180°C for 35 minutes. To serve, dredge the tops with icing sugar and serve warm with crème anglaise.

SERVES 6

Sweet Cannoli with Summer Berries The cannoli 'forms' (cylinder-shaped) required for this recipe can be purchased from specialist kitchen shops.

380g plain flour

4 tablespoons butter

1 egg

2 egg yolks

water (if required)

vegetable oil

Place the flour and butter in a food processor and pulse together until the mixture resembles fine breadcrumbs. Add the egg, egg yolks and enough water to process the mixture to form a ball of dough. Wrap in plastic food wrap and refrigerate for 30 minutes. Roll out the pastry on a lightly floured board to about 10mm thick. Cut into 10cm squares and wrap the squares around a cylinder or cannoli forms.

Deep-fry in preheated hot vegetable oil for about 30 seconds in batches of 3–4 at a time, moving the forms as they cook. Remove the cannoli gently from the oil with tongs. Remove the forms using another pair of tongs and return the cannoli to the oil for a further 30 seconds to cook the insides. Drain on absorbent kitchen paper and allow to cool.

FILLING

300g fresh ricotta cheese

200g mascarpone

2 tablespoons icing sugar

$^1/_4$ cup toasted almonds, finely chopped

1 tablespoon cassis (blackcurrant) liqueur

fresh summer berries

icing sugar

Blend the ricotta, mascarpone and icing sugar together to form a paste. Stir in the toasted chopped almonds and cassis. Pipe the filling into the cooled cannoli shells. Serve with a small pile of fruit and dredge the cannoli and fruit with a little icing sugar.

MAKES 12

staples

Plum and Apple Chutney

6 large apples (about 1kg), peeled and diced

8 red-fleshed plums, pitted and diced

2 medium onions, peeled and finely chopped

2 cloves garlic, crushed

1 cup raisins, chopped

2 teaspoons grated fresh ginger

$1/2$ teaspoon ground nutmeg

1 teaspoon ground cinnamon

1 fresh red chilli, deseeded and finely chopped

1 teaspoon grated orange zest

1 cup orange juice

1 teaspoon grated lemon zest

juice of 1 lemon

3 cups white vinegar

2 cups brown sugar

Combine the fruit, onions, garlic, raisins, spices, chilli, zest, juice and vinegar in a large heavy-bottomed saucepan. Bring to the boil and simmer, uncovered, for about 40 minutes or until the mixture is thick. Remove from the heat and stir in the brown sugar. Stir over a gentle heat, without boiling, until the sugar has dissolved. Return to simmering point and continue to cook for about 1 hour, uncovered. Stir occasionally. When the mixture is thick, pour into hot sterilised jars. Seal when cold. Keeps for up to 12 months.

MAKES 6 X 250G JARS

Sherry Vinaigrette

50ml sherry vinegar

300ml extra virgin olive oil

juice of $1/2$ lemon

sea salt and freshly ground black pepper
    to taste

2–3 tablespoons water

Whisk all ingredients together.

MAKES ABOUT 1 $1/2$ CUPS

Vanilla Sugar

2 fresh, moist vanilla pods

500g caster sugar

Cut the vanilla pods into small pieces. Place the pods and caster sugar in a food processor and pulse together until the sugar is ash-coloured. Sieve the mixture, return the vanilla lumps to the food processor, pulse again and add them to the rest of the sugar. Store in an airtight container. Add to cream or mascarpone, sprinkle over baked fruits etc.

MAKES 2 CUPS

Red Pepper Relish

4 large red peppers (capsicums)

2 onions, peeled and coarsely chopped

1 large fresh red chilli, deseeded

3 cloves garlic, peeled

2 cups white vinegar

about 7 cups sugar

sea salt to taste

2 kaffir lime leaves

1 bay leaf

Slice around the core of the red peppers, remove any white membrane and roughly chop the flesh. In batches, place the red peppers, onions, chilli and garlic in a food processor and pulse until smooth. Transfer to a heavy-bottomed saucepan. Add the vinegar and simmer for 20 minutes. Pour the mixture into a measuring jug to establish the quantity made. Add an equal amount of sugar and return both to the saucepan. Stir until the sugar dissolves, then return to a gentle boil. Season to taste with salt, and add the kaffir lime leaves and bay leaf. Stir occasionally. Simmer for 30 minutes or until it looks thick, removing any scum with a metal spoon.

Remove the lime and bay leaves. Spoon the relish into warm, clean jars, seal and store in a cool, dark place for up to a year. After opening it will keep in the refrigerator for up to 6 weeks.

MAKES 5 CUPS

Onion Relish

2kg brown onions, peeled, halved and finely sliced

100ml olive oil

2 tablespoons grated fresh ginger

$1/2$ teaspoon ground mixed spice

freshly ground black pepper to taste

$3^1/2$ cups brown sugar, tightly packed

1 cup balsamic vinegar

$1/2$ cup red wine vinegar

1 bay leaf

In a heavy-bottomed saucepan cook the onions with the olive oil over a low heat until soft. Add the ginger, mixed spice, black pepper, brown sugar, vinegars and bay leaf and stir until the sugar dissolves. Bring to a gentle boil and simmer for 40 minutes or until thick and syrupy, removing the scum as it appears. Remove the bay leaf. Spoon the onion relish into clean warm jars and seal. Store in a cool, dark place for up to 1 year. Once opened, store in the refrigerator.

MAKES ABOUT 6 CUPS

Lemon Mayonnaise

2 egg yolks

$1^3/4$ cups olive oil

4–5 tablespoons lemon juice

sea salt to taste

Place the egg yolks in a food processor or blender. With the motor running, begin adding the olive oil, drop by drop, until the mixture thickens to form an emulsion. Add a tablespoon of lemon juice and continue to add the olive oil in a slow, steady thin stream. Add extra lemon juice to taste and adjust the thickness. Season to taste with salt. Use within 2 weeks.

MAKES 2 CUPS

weights & measures

Abbreviations

g	gram
kg	kilogram
mm	millimetre
cm	centimetre
ml	millilitre
°C	degrees Celsius

Weight conversions

NZ METRIC	IMPERIAL/US
25g	1 oz
50g	2 oz
75g	3 oz
100g	$3^1/_2$ oz
125g	$4^1/_2$ oz
150g	5 oz
175g	6 oz
200g	7 oz
225g	8 oz
250g	9 oz
275g	$9^1/_2$ oz
300g	$10^1/_2$ oz
325g	$11^1/_2$ oz
350g	$12^1/_2$ oz
375g	13 oz
400g	14 oz
450g	16 oz (1 lb)
500g	$17^1/_2$ oz
750g	$26^1/_2$ oz
1 kg	35 oz ($2^1/_4$ lb)

Length conversions

METRIC	IMPERIAL/US
0.5cm (5mm)	$^1/_4$ inch
1cm	$^1/_2$ inch
2.5cm	1 inch
5cm	2 inches
10cm	4 inches
20cm	8 inches
30cm	12 inches (1 foot)

Liquid conversions

NZ METRIC	IMPERIAL	US
5ml (1 teaspoon)	$^1/_4$ fl oz	1 teaspoon
15ml (1 tablespoon)	$^1/_2$ fl oz	1 tablespoon
30ml ($^1/_8$ cup)	1 fl oz	$^1/_8$ cup
60ml ($^1/_4$ cup)	2 fl oz	$^1/_4$ cup
125ml ($^1/_2$ cup)	4 fl oz	$^1/_2$ cup
150ml	5 fl oz ($^1/_4$ pint)	$^2/_3$ cup
175ml	6 fl oz	$^3/_4$ cup
250ml (1 cup)	8 fl oz	1 cup ($^1/_2$ pint)
300ml	10 fl oz ($^1/_2$ pint)	1 $^1/_4$ cups
375ml	12 fl oz	1 $^1/_2$ cups
500ml (2 cups)	16 fl oz	2 cups (1 pint)
600ml	20 fl oz (1 pint)	2 $^1/_2$ cups

NB The Australian metric tablespoon measures 20ml

Temperature conversions

CELSIUS	FAHRENHEIT	GAS
100°C	225°F	1/4
125°C	250°F	1/2
150°C	300°F	2
160°C	325°F	3
170°C	325°F	3
180°C	350°F	4
190°C	375°F	5
200°C	400°F	6
210°C	425°F	7
220°C	425°F	7
230°C	450°F	8
250°C	500°F	9

Cake tin sizes

METRIC	IMPERIAL/US
15cm	6 inches
18cm	7 inches
20cm	8 inches
23cm	9 inches
25cm	10 inches
28cm	11 inches

index

acknowledgements

Thank you so much Renée Lang, Belinda Cooke and the team at New Holland Publishers for their support, friendship and dedication to excellence as always. Christine Hansen, yet again, has produced an inspired book design to showcase our pleasurable work. To my fantastic editor, Barbara Nielsen, thanks for being such a pleasant policewoman. Family and friends as usual were reliable, and positive critics and testers were ever ready with spoons. Thank you one and all. My co-author Ian Batchelor, who creates the glorious food images, has once again outdone himself. I hope my readers have as much fun and laughs creating the recipes as I did styling them and Ian did shooting them.

Penny Oliver

suppliers

Nest Homewares, Newmarket, Auckland
Country Road Homewares, Newmarket, Auckland
Superb Herb Co. Ltd